SPIRITUAL
COVID

The Legitimate Church Is Waking Up

WAYNE KNIFFEN

WESTBOW
PRESS®
A DIVISION OF THOMAS NELSON
& ZONDERVAN

WestBow Press books may be ordered through booksellers or by contacting:

WestBow Press
A Division of Thomas Nelson & Zondervan
1663 Liberty Drive
Bloomington, IN 47403
www.westbowpress.com
844-714-3454

ISBN: 979-8-3850-0012-8 (sc)
ISBN: 979-8-3850-0013-5 (hc)
ISBN: 979-8-3850-0014-2 (e)

Library of Congress Control Number: 2023914313

Print information available on the last page.

WestBow Press rev. date: 07/27/2023

This book is dedicated to the memory of
Dr. John H. Beard
(a.k.a. Brother Johnny)

Brother Johnny had a positive influence on my life and on many young preacher boys. Brother Johnny help me work through my Vietnam experience; he baptized me; he gave me invaluable counsel when I surrendered my life to the gospel ministry, and he ordained me when I was called to my first pastorate. He was always available and willing to listen no matter what time of day or night. Brother Johnny put his thumbprint on a lot of people, especially young preacher boys.

What he left will continue to live on. I
am determined to do the same.
"Thank you, Beloved."

CONTENTS

Preface ix

Chapter 1   Spiritual COVID Syndrome 1
Chapter 2   A Glimpse of the Last-Season Church 22
Chapter 3   A Season of Expectation 35
Chapter 4   The Church Is Waking Up 51
Chapter 5   Resurgence of the Small Home Church 68
Chapter 6   Lessons From Uganda 83
Chapter 7   Immunity from Spiritual COVID 97
Chapter 8   The Most Dangerous Warning Sign of All 116

About the Author 137

PREFACE

During the summer of 2018, I noticed several places in my front yard where the grass was dying. These dead spots seemed to be expanding exponentially. After a considerable amount of time meditating on my lawn problem, I came up with a plan to deal with this growing cancer. I would continue to irrigate my yard by using the sprinkler system, then I would take the water hose and saturate each dead spot with water. One day as I was soaking these dead spots of grass with vengeance, these words went off in my spirit: *Water what's alive, and it will overtake what has died.* I remember the aha moment that flashed through my spirit as if it were yesterday. I knew these words had more significance than just watering dead spots in my front yard where the grass was not growing. I just did not know how much more.

Water what is alive, and it will overtake what has died. It would be advantageous for us to pay attention to these instructions because we spend an inordinate amount of time, energy, and resources watering *lifeless spots* in our lives that seemingly have died. We have convinced ourselves that if we can get enough water applied to these areas, things will come to life again. What we need to do is give our attention to watering what is alive and thriving in our lives. If we will do this, it will not be long before what is alive will begin to overtake what has died. Life will always overpower death.

I am so thankful that I shared this aha moment with my wife. I also shared it with a good pastor friend of mine and with my Tuesday morning pastor's group. When these words went off in my spirit, I knew it was a *now word*. I just did not know how *now* it was! It is the key that unlocks the prophetic vision I received a year later. This is why I am so thankful I went on record and shared it when it happened.

A prophetic vision was given to me on January 28, 2019. I saw a large area that had been devastated by fire. My total focus was on the trees and vegetation that had been destroyed. I remember having feelings of deep sadness as I looked at the charred debris left by the fire. As I stood there gazing at the destruction, I heard these words in my innermost being: "Don't focus on what has been burned (sounds familiar). If you do, the enemy wins. Pay attention to the green, lush, new life emerging. This was not a wildfire; it was a controlled burn. What has been burned are the things in which you have found security. A new is arising. Out of the old, the new is springing up. What has been burned is making way for the new that could not be seen before the fire. The new has always been there. The old has prepared you for the new, which will be your final and most productive season. The fire is what I have allowed to release your passion, compulsion, zeal, creativity, and motivation. The loss the fire caused has released you to do what I have had in mind for you since the beginning of time. It took the fire to get your undivided attention. Because it was a controlled burn, the real you has not suffered loss. This was not a wildfire."

My preaching ministry began in August 1973 at the age of twenty-five. That was fifty years ago. I am now seventy-four years young. Some people who used to be my friends have told me that I am now the same age as old people: Maybe so, maybe not. There is one thing for sure; I am in my last season in this physical realm. It has been an incredibly productive one too, just like the Lord said it would be. In a period of two-and-a-half-years, He has helped me write twelve books. This was accomplished while we were in the middle of a COVID pandemic that has not only affected the United States; it has touched the entire globe. It would be hard to find anybody who does not know somebody who has not been infected or affected by this virus. I think my choice of words to describe this season that we find ourselves in right now would be: weird. When you think things cannot get any weirder, they do.

I am convinced this COVID fire is part and parcel of the controlled burn I saw in my prophetic vision. Our natural response is to lock in on what has been destroyed by fire and not see the new that is emerging because of the fire. What has been burned is making way for the new that could not be seen before the burn. Out of the old the new is springing up. I firmly believe that we have entered the greatest season of our lives. In no way am I making light of people's personal losses, especially the loss of life that so many have experienced. That is heart-wrenching. I have preached memorial services during this pandemic where family members were not allowed to attend their own loved one's service. It is not natural when a wife cannot attend the funeral service of her husband and vice versa.

My wife and I have experienced our share of loss during this season as well. At times we have struggled to stay on our feet. With the help of the Holy Spirit and the sensitive hearts of dear friends, we are still standing. We know firsthand what Paul meant when he said, "I know things will turn out okay for me through the provision of the Spirit and the prayers of the Saints" (Philippians 1:19; my personal paraphrase).

What is true in our personal lives is also true in the life of the church. Today the church can rise and be everything God intended for it to be. A controlled burn is going on within the church. This controlled burn is not to destroy the church, because the church cannot be destroyed, but to release the church to be what the Lord had in mind since the beginning. It has taken the fire to get our undivided attention. The true church is rising in power and with purpose. The church may be in its final season here on the earth, but more can be accomplished in these last days than we can imagine. We just need to be aware of what is going on and redeem the time.

What Joseph said to his brothers is appropriate for this season in which we find ourselves. "You intended to harm me, but God intended it all for good. He brought me to this position so I could save the lives of many people" (Genesis 50:20 NLT). Whatever the enemy uses in his attempt to destroy us, God uses to deliver us. Everything the enemy uses in his effort to weaken us God uses to strengthen us. The body of Christ is not only rising; the church is coming alive in the power of its true identity.

During this pandemic, many people who have struggled with this potentially fatal disease have had to be intubated. Intubation is placing a tube in a person's throat to help move air in and out of his or her lungs. The purpose of intubation is to open the airway to give oxygen, anesthesia and medicine, to remove blockages, and to help a person breathe if he or she has collapsed lungs, heart failure, or trauma.

Keep this definition of intubation in mind as you think about the church. Is it possible that God has had his church intubated so he can get her healthy and ready for his last-day assignment? I have been intimately involved with the church for approximately fifty-two years. That is not a long time in comparison to how long the church has been in existence. And I am not presenting myself as an authority on church history. That is not the purpose of this book.

I am speaking out of my experience as a pastor of local churches for many, many years. I see the church differently now than I did when I first started, which has made me love the church even more. If you want to get yourself in dutch with the Lord, talk about or be rude to his children: Things will not end well.

Over the last half-century, I have seen glimpses of what the church can do—what it should look and act like. But there has not been much consistency or longevity in these seasons. The church has had moments when it flexed its spiritual muscles and impacted parts of the world in incredible ways, but humanity has always found a way to stifle the movement of the Spirit. Here is the good news. What God is raising and empowering is not a denomination, a particular ministry, or the ecclesiastical establishment. God is bringing the true church out of the bed of religion and status quo. She will never again fall into a state of slumber and lethargy. The enemy will not be able to silence her voice; nor will the gates of hell be able to stop the church in these last days (Matthew 16:18 NKJV). God will see to it.

This is not a time to be a spectator. Those days are over. It is time to rise and become a participator. God wants to use you in ways you never dreamed possible. Age and gender are not a limitation either. You may have to experience a controlled burn so the things that you have found security in are no longer available to you. I assure you, it will not be comfortable, but it will be freeing. If you are a child of God, you are living in the most exciting of times. If you are not a child of God, this would be a good time to get that settled by accepting and receiving Jesus Christ as your personal Lord and Savior.

We have entered the season where God is going to reveal that every church is not the Lord's church, but the Lord has his church in every church. The church is coming out of intubation. Miracles, signs, and wonders will be following those who believe (Mark 16:17 NKJV). God is going to take those of us who want to participate out of our comfort zones into zones where the Holy Spirit is our only comfort (2 Corinthians 1:3–4 NKJV). The supernatural is going to become natural to those who have the audacity to believe and to those who expect it. "The people who know their God shall be strong, and carry out great exploits" (Daniel 11:32 NKJV).

SPIRITUAL COVID
SYNDROME

H ave we made the church to be something that it was never intended to be? Should we be more interested in gathering and keeping people or in releasing and sending them out? What is our motivation for reaching more people? I think most of us would agree that to send people out, we must get people in. But it is possible to do both. I am afraid we lean more to the side of gathering people, with the intent of keeping them, than we do sending them out. To answer these questions, all we must do is take a hard look at a church's budget. What we will discover is that most churches are spending more time, energy, and resources on building bigger crowds and doing whatever it takes to add to our attendance. Absolutely nothing is wrong with that if our intent is to mature them in the faith so they can be sent out to share it with others. Maybe we have gotten to the point where our priorities are not where they should be. Today, far too many churches are placing more emphasis on building bigger crowds, constructing more buildings, and buying more land than sending people out so they can share their faith with a lost and dying world. The question that every serious-minded leader in the church should ask themselves is "Why do I want more people?"

Gathering people is not a bad thing in and of itself. What we need to seriously wrestle with is why we are so bent toward filling our "religious mausoleums" with more people. Maybe head count has taken precedence over what really counts.

In writing to the church at Corinth, Paul uses the analogy of the human body to help us understand the spiritual body—the church (1 Corinthians 12:1–31 NKJV). For the human body to remain healthy, there must be the expulsion of waste matter so toxins can be eliminated. Excretion is an essential process in all living things. It helps to prevent damage to the body. It is one of the major ways the human body maintains homeostasis. Without the ability to eliminate toxins, the body will bloat, and it will create complications. It is the process of the body taking in, processing what has been taken in, and then releasing. This is what I want you to focus on. For our bodies to be healthy, there must be a balance of inflow and outflow.

What is true concerning the physical body also applies to the spiritual body that we call the church. A healthy church will focus on reaching, teaching, and releasing people. We reach people so we can teach and mature them in their new creation identities in Christ. The motivation behind teaching the people we have reached should be on sending them out to reach more people. The ones we are sending out allow us to expand the kingdom. If our motivation for reaching more people is so we can send more people out, we may find ourselves the recipients of divine intervention and resources to help us reach more people. God will always make sure that we have adequate provision to carry out his vision. We have gotten fairly efficient at reaching and teaching people, but we still have some work to do when it comes to releasing people.

I spent the first twenty-seven years of my ministry pastoring churches that were a part of a particular denomination. My experience pastoring these churches was incredible. I would not trade anything for that season in my life. For the last twenty-three years, I've pastored a church that is not a part of a particular denomination.

We are an autonomous group, but we have chosen to be in fellowship with other churches of like-mindedness and spiritual affinity.

I still have some dear friends who pastor churches in the denomination that I was a part of for so long. Many of them have already retired. We stay in contact with one another, and I am blessed to have them as friends. I am deeply appreciative to that denomination for making sure that I was grounded in the Word of God and for instilling in me a burning desire to see souls come to know Christ. Today we have too many leaders and churches who are a mile wide and an inch deep.

During the twenty-seven years that I pastored a denominational church, I attended my share of conferences where most attendees were from the same denomination. When you are being introduced to someone for the first time, within the first few minutes of the introduction exchange, you will be asked this question: "How many people are attending your services?" This is one question you can always rely on being asked. The number of people that are attending your church has become the criteria used by the ecclesiastical hierarchy to measure a pastor's effectiveness and success. This is sad but true. Most pastors are convinced that the larger the number of people attending their church services is what determines their success or their failure. Value and self-worth, is moored to the size of how many people are in attendance. The more people you gather, the greater your value. This was certainly not the motive of every person who asked this question, but these are the words the enemy will use to attack a pastor's self-worth. After all, we live in a ministry culture where bigger is synonymous with being better. Don't shout me down.

The number of people who attend Sunday services has become the financial engine that drives the ministry of the average local church. The more people you can gather in your Sunday morning Bible classes, the greater the financial impact it will have on the bottom line of your budget. Most local churches have already figured out what it costs per head to open the front doors of the church building. A dollar value is placed on every person who attends. Those in leadership positions may never tell the folks in the pew what it costs per person to open the doors, but I assure you, most church leadership teams know. There is a business side to any ministry, but when the business side begins to outweigh the ministry side, it is a sure setup to have a form of godliness but not true power. When more money is spent on salaries, buildings, upkeep, and maintenance than on missions and sending people out, we have a symptom of spiritual COVID. It makes it difficult to do what the Holy Spirit wants us to do when we must consider what our overhead expenses are before we can say yes to what God told us to do.

Again, I am in no way saying or insinuating that every church and every church leader has ulterior motives for gathering large crowds of people. I firmly believe that most church leadership teams are godly men and women who make incredible sacrifices every day to make sure the kingdom of God advances. I am not painting with a broad brush. What I am encouraging is that all of us who claim to be followers of Jesus Christ, whether we stand in the pulpit or sit in the pew, honestly wrestle with the questions we are raising. Why do we do what we do, the way we do? If the church has been intubated for a season, and I'm convinced it has, we need to know why.

Here is a side note. Have you ever seen a brochure or a poster promoting a Bible conference or any meeting without a picture of the speaker(s) and these words underneath: "Bro. No Name, pastor of the First Forgotten Church, Somewhere. They average sixty-five people in their weekly service"? I have never seen one either, because they don't exist. We cannot print posters and flyers promoting our conferences and meetings without emphasizing the number of people the speakers are gathering or how many church campuses the guest speakers are overseeing. Numbers have become our standard for ministry success. Why is this? I think the answer is obvious. Our culture believes that bigger is always better.

Attending conferences did not end when I became the pastor of a nondenominational church. But there was one noticeable difference.

When I was introduced to someone, they never asked me how many we had attending our Sunday morning Bible studies or how many we had in our church services. What I did hear was something like this: "What is God saying to you? Where do you think God is taking you?" I cannot tell you how refreshing that is to hear. In no way am I saying or implying that one group is more spiritual than the other one. That is alien to my thinking. It does reveal that whatever we are exposed to for any length of time has a way of getting entwined into our thinking.

After several years of pastoring a nondenominational church, I had a flashback moment that took me back to my roots. In one of our meetings, I was being introduced to a guy I had never met. His first words to me were, "How many do you run in Sunday school?" I will have to admit, his question caught me off guard. I had not been asked that question in several years. Here is what came out of my mouth before I gave it any thought: "How long did you pastor in the _____?" (I named the denomination.) His facial expression was priceless. The sign on his face read, "How in the world do you know that?" I never told him. I let him think that I had a special hotline to the Holy Spirit that he did not have. I know what you are probably thinking. I have repented. Sometimes my greatest accomplishment is keeping my mouth shut.

WE HAVE TAUGHT OUR BROTHERS WELL

I've had the opportunity to travel all over the world ministering on who we are as new creations in Christ. This has given me the honor to preach in some unique places. The most memorable place I have ever preached, without hesitation, was in the garden of Gethsemane in Israel. I preached "The Exchanged Life" message in the proximity of where Jesus poured out his soul just before he went to the whipping post, then to the cross. That once-in-a-lifetime moment will always have a special place in my heart.

Three other places are forever etched in my memory. The opportunity I had in Uganda was nothing short of phenomenal. I will talk about this incredible experience in greater depth and length in the chapters to follow. The other two places would have to be Kenya and Mexico. Some of the places in these countries are so remote that I'm not sure the Lord knew where we were. I say that tongue-in-cheek. If something nefarious had happened to us at either place, it would have taken years for anyone to find out about it—if ever.

What is striking to me is that in Uganda and Kenya the church services we attended were conducted just like we do here in America. How did they learn to do church this way? When we talked to the local pastors and church leadership teams, their desires and aspirations were the same as American pastors: buy more land, build bigger facilities, and gather more people. We have taught our brothers and sisters well.

THE BACK ROADS OF KENYA

We drove and drove; then we drove some more. I thought we would never arrive at the church where we had been assigned to preach. The narrow dirt road we had been traveling on had turned into a path—a very narrow one, too. Finely, we came to a small building that was big enough to hold approximately fifty people, but over one hundred people were jammed inside. I have no clue where all these people came from. We had not seen a house or village for miles.

The temperature had just inched past 110 degrees when we pulled up to the building where this gathering was taking place. The pastor was outside with his entourage, robing up. That is not a misread. He was putting on clothes, and I was wanting to take some of my clothes off. Did I mention it was hot? After receiving specific instructions about the proper protocol for the service, it came time for us to enter the building. We were lined up in order of rank; the pastor being first, then his elders and me, followed by others who were leaders in the church. We solemnly marched inside single file to be seated at our designated places up front. The people stood as we entered the building and did not sit down until we sat down. I noticed that no one was smiling. No joy was present. None. The entire service was cold and sterile in every aspect. I remember thinking to myself, *We are in the deep bowels of Kenya. How did they learn to do church this way?*

To this day I have no clue what the pastor read from. It certainly was not the scriptures. I thought he would never finish. After he concluded his lengthy read, he introduced me. I stood and began to minister the word that I felt the Lord had given me. At first it was like preaching on the wrong side of a cold, dark tomb. Not a flicker of life was present. Finally, I stopped and asked for the pastor's permission to invite the children to the front where I was. He graciously gave me his consent. When all the children had gathered around me, I continued my message. I spoke to the adults through the children, as if I were talking only to the little ones. Even though the adults were my primary audience, I pretended they were not in the building. When we involved the innocence of children in the service, the Spirit of God began to move, and we witnessed some incredible things. All we did was make a slight shift from doing things a little different than they had always been done—something most churches have an aversion to. We can do what we do for so long that we think it is the only way things can be done.

WHERE THE JUNGLE AND THE CHURCH MET

I have had the opportunity preach in Mexico on numerous occasions. It also happens to be one of my favorite places to minister. I know what you are probably thinking, every place is his favorite place to preach. Guilty as charged. The Mexican people have been gracious and very welcoming. But I had never been to where we were going on this one trip. From where we started, it took our team almost four hours to get to a town that I have been told is the oldest continually inhabited city in Mexico; dating back some twenty-five-hundred years. The name of this town is Cholula, home of some of the best hot sauce I have ever tasted. The south end of this small town ended where the jungle began. It was a fascinating experience. The service did not have more than twenty-five people in attendance, but it was full of life, and everyone was engaged with what was going on. The music was lively, and the people were animated in their worship of the Lord. The Spirit of God was so obviously present that it made us forget about the primitive environment we were in. The people were full of life, and you could tell the joy of the Lord was their strength.

A small boy was sitting in a chair on the front row to my immediate right. I am guessing he was six or seven years old. I watched him during our time of praise and worship. He was uninhibited in his worship: He was very expressive. When it came time for me to minister the word, I was going to ask him his name and then talk about how inspiring it was to watch him worship. When I turned to look at him, I noticed his chair was empty. I asked the people what his name was and if anyone knew where he went. Everyone said his name in unison and then pointed. When I turned to look in the direction that they were pointing, I saw him. He was standing no more than twenty feet away relieving himself. The south side of the building that we were in was open to the river and the jungle. When I called his name, he looked at me over his shoulder and smiled. That is a boy for you: another moment that was added to my treasure trove of special memories.

Where did the people in this jungle-town in Mexico learn to do church? The thing that I want you to understand is that no matter where you go, whether it be Uganda, Kenya, Mexico, or wherever, you will find people expressing themselves in church just like you will find here in America. Some are very warm and expressive while others are cold and sterile. Whether they are hot or cold, the primary focus of every church that I've ministered in has been the same. The leadership wants to gather more people, buy more land, and build bigger buildings.

I found an exception in Juarez, Mexico. Pastor José Munoz is a breath of fresh air. He is always looking for ways to expand the kingdom of God. He is constantly sending out men and women from his church who feel God's call on their lives to places where they can gather people, mature them in the faith, then send them out. His heart is to release people to serve. Here is an interesting statistic. The more he sends out, the more he can gather. What motivates Pastor José' is not gathering more people; it's sending more people out. This is a rare commodity found in the church today. We need more leaders like this man.

SPIRITUAL COVID SYMPTOMS

Symptoms of spiritual COVID have been present in the church for a while, and for the most part, the church has not been aware of it. This contagious disease has spread to the church worldwide. It has taken this controlled burn season to expose the spiritual condition of the church for the purpose of getting it healthy.

The church has brought this spiritual virus upon itself because of poor spiritual hygiene. For the church to be healthy and strong for her last-day assignments, it was necessary for the church to be intubated. Here is the good news. The church is coming out of intubation. The true church is rising in power and strength in its identity in Christ. Like Samson, the church is shaking off unbelief and doubt and will do what it has been empowered to do from the very beginning—to prepare the world for the return of the King of kings and the Lord of lords.

This spiritual COVID syndrome is why we (the church) don't expect or believe that God will perform miracles, signs, and wonders among us. We are convinced that *"this kind of stuff"* is relegated to third world countries where options are limited, and the people are largely ignorant. Here is a news flash: It is not about us having options. We do not see supernatural moves of God in our weekly gatherings because we have been crippled and weakened by a spiritual COVID virus causing us not to expect or believe things like this will happen here.

Here are six spiritual COVID symptoms that have infected and affected the church. We have chosen doing over being, human ability over divine anointing, personality over character, talent over spiritual gifting, positive thinking over faith, and man's opinion over God's word. Let's examine each symptom separately.

DOING OVER BEING

The church has stressed doing over being. There is certainly a place for doing in the family of faith, but it should not be at the expense of being. Our doing (what we do) should come out of our being (who we are). We should never get trapped into thinking that what we are doing determines who we are. Who we are should determine what we do. The fruit that is produced by substituting doing for being is tainted. Once we consume this contaminated fruit, we become anemic. When our spiritual immune system is compromised, we become susceptible to even more dangerous symptoms.

This is why there are so many quitters and pretenders in the church today. When people are focused on doing over being, it does not take long before they get tired and worn out. Burnout is inevitable. When this happens, people will either quit assembling with the community of faith, or they will start pretending. They are not okay, but they want you to think all is well. Pretenders may continue being a part of the praise team, serving as greeters, attending services, even giving their money, but their hearts left the building a long time ago. Doing lovely things for God is not the same thing as being in love with God.

When we focus on who we are as new creations in Christ, we will be active, but our works will be flowing out of our identities. We were created as human beings not human doings. The motivation behind what we are doing is not for the purpose of obtaining our new creation identities. People who learn how to walk out their new creation identity will accomplish more than they would ever accomplish in the flesh, and they will not quit or become pretenders when things become difficult.

"For we are His workmanship, *created in Christ Jesus for good works*, which God *prepared beforehand that we should walk in them*" (Ephesians 2:10 NKJV; emphasis added). Paul makes it crystal clear that every child of God is his masterpiece, created for good works. These good works have been set before us (prepared beforehand). When we live our daily lives in the awareness that we are in union with Christ, we will naturally do (work) the works that God has set before us. We will never have to wonder if we are doing what God wants us to do. Since we are walking with the One who set the good works before us, we can be confident that He will lead us in doing these good works. Our doing (works) will come out of our being (who we are).

Because the church has opted for doing over being, it has had to be spiritually intubated so it can regain its health for this last season of being the Lord's church. The body of Christ is rising and coming out of intubation.

HUMAN ABILITY OVER DIVINE ANOINTING

Once doing becomes more important to the church than being, it is only natural for the church to settle for human ability instead of divine anointing. Because human ability can give us our desired results, we have no problem accepting ability over anointing. I am sure you have heard it said about some great athlete that he or she is a natural talent, or the person has natural ability. Natural ability is a great way to define human talent because that is exactly what it is—natural. Ability is being able to accomplish and do things well. When something is accomplished by one's own ability, he or she gets the recognition and credit for it.

Because the church has had measured success in gathering people, we have filled our facilities with religious athletes who are endowed with natural ability. I cannot tell you how many times I have watched these religious athletes perform in their assigned ministry roles in heroic proportions, then begin to drift and fall away. They cannot be found today, even with the assistance of the FBI and the CIA. Unless our understanding changes, and we get healthy, we will replace them with another gifted athlete who has natural ability. And the never-ending cycle continues. This happens because we have settled for human ability over divine anointing.

Anointing, on the other hand, is the manifest presence of God empowering an individual to accomplish a certain task or to do things that are beyond one's human ability. John writes, "But you have an anointing from the Holy One, and you know all things" (1 John 2:20 NKJV). Fresh anointing is what makes the difference in our prayers, our praise, and in our personal lives. The church needs a big anointing for this last-day season. You can fake ability for a while, but you cannot fake anointing. Ability is a man-made substitute for anointing. It is fake. If we are doing what we do out of human ability, a time will come when we struggle in trying to do the will of God. We flow when we do what we do in the empowerment of the anointing.

In no way am I suggesting malfeasance on the part of those who are responsible for staffing ministry positions within the church. I am convinced it is done out of ignorance and unhealthy expectations the people have placed on their leaders. After all, success means bigger is always better. To get bigger, we must have a strategy to gather more people. That in and of itself is not wrong, if our motivation for gathering more people is to mature them in their faith in Christ with the intent of sending them out. Our heavenly mandate is not solely on gathering people. Our marching orders are to send people out so they can gather people and mature them in their new creation identities, so they can be sent out.

Wouldn't it be refreshing when being introduced to someone, that the first question asked after the name exchange was, "How many have you sent out this year?" I bet you would get one of those looks. You know what I am saying.

The life of the church has become routine. We are very predictable. This last season that we are in will require the church to be healthy, innovative, bold, expectant, and willing to take dominion in this earthly realm—Genesis 1:26–28 has not been repealed. There is no way the church will be able to carry out its assignment in this last season if it remains in its present condition—and it will not. The power of the anointing brings freshness to everything. The entire atmosphere can be affected by God's anointing.

During a Sunday morning service our choir was singing that great song written by Gloria and Bill Gather, "It Is Finished." At the crescendo point of this song about the return of Christ, the kettledrums rumbled. Instantly, the entire congregation rose to their feet simultaneously. No one orchestrated it. It was like a huge hand was placed underneath the entire worship center and lifted everyone to their feet. It was one of those divine moments when heaven touched earth. The anointing had affected the entire atmosphere of the worship service.

Sometime later, the choir sang this song again. It was magnificent, but the moment was different. At the very same spot where we had that divine encounter weeks earlier, someone stood and began to motion for others to stand. People all over the building began to stand. It was not a bad thing, but it was obvious that moment was orchestrated by the flesh and not by the Spirit. If we are sensitive to the things of the Spirit, we should always be able to recognize when things are done in the strength of one's ability or in the power of divine anointing. We are spiritual beings after all.

When something is done in the power of the anointing, God gets the glory and credit. God wants to empower his church with his anointing so the world can see that He can take anybody and make them somebody who can bless everybody. This is the heart of our heavenly Father.

PERSONALITY OVER CHARACTER

When the church accepts human ability over divine anointing, the next symptom that manifests is that we will settle for personality over character. We have plenty of characters in the church, but what we need are more individuals who have character. Personality is who people think we are. Character is who we really are.

When the church looks for someone to fill a staff position, someone with a good personality and natural ability will usually be chosen over someone with character. And it is not because leadership teams believe personality is the most important thing; it is because personality can be recognized instantly where it may take time and experience to recognize character. Time is not something we think we have. Is it possible to have both personality and character? Absolutely! Since we are usually in a hurry to fill vacant positions (we've got to gather more people) our proclivity is to gravitate to someone's personality much faster than taking the time to discover a person's character.

Humanly speaking, a great personality who has natural ability will usually be a church's person of choice. This person is so likeable, and certainly has the ability, so we believe that he or she will be able to accomplish more. What we stand to forfeit is character, divine anointing, and integrity. And these are the attributes that are needed in this last-season assignment.

The church is waking up. It is coming out of intubation. In this last season before Christ returns, the legitimate church will be living out its new creation identity. There will still be religious gatherings, but they will be going through the motions. Their services will continue to be sterile religious exercises, just like that one church I told you about in Kenya. The true church will be demonstrating the power of God, in word and deed, to a lost and hopeless world.

Character and integrity are inseparable. Trying to separate the two would be like trying to separate water from wetness. A person with character will be a person of integrity. A person who has integrity will be a person of character. Integrity is the quality of being honest and having strong moral principles. Integrity is the state of being whole and undivided.

Why is character and integrity more important than personality and natural ability? People have always been watching those who claim to be Christians, but in this last season the world will scrutinize what a person claims to be more than ever. The world is hurting, and they desperately need answers, so they will be looking for legitimate believers. What are they seeing?

The world is looking for believers whose behavior matches what they say they believe. The reason a person behaves wrong is because he or she believes wrong. If we believe right, we will behave right. It is possible to deceive oneself by thinking, *I know I may not be living right, but at least I believe right.* That's self-deception. We have a behavior issue, not only in the world but also within the church, because we have a belief issue. The world is looking for people who not only believe right; they are looking for individuals who behave right.

The world is looking for believers whose walk matches their talk. People with personality and natural ability may talk the talk, but are they walking the walk? It is one thing to talk a good game; it is another to live it. In this last season, people are looking for those abnormal believers—the ones who not only say they believe in the power of God but who also are living in the power of God. What we proclaim on Sunday, we practice on Monday.

The world is looking for believers whose character matches their confession. People of character and integrity will be the same in their private lives as they are in their public lives. Their faith is not a style of living, always changing to keep in step with what is *WOKE*: Their faith is a lifestyle. A style of living is living life from the outside in. A lifestyle is living life from the inside out. A person of character and integrity will make healthy and sound choices even when it is not popular with the status quo.

When I answered God's call on my life back in the early 1970s, I was told that Christians are like tea bags; you really do not know what is inside of them until they are placed in hot water. Hot-water experiences are what God uses to reveal if a person has character or if he or she is just a character.

TALENT OVER SPIRITUAL GIFTING

When the church settles for personality over character, the next symptom that manifests is talent over spiritual gifting. The local church has been in a steady downward spiral for years because we have substituted what God has for the church for what is expedient and for what has produced our desired results. The church is looking for those who are talented at the expense of spiritual giftings. God gave spiritual gifts to the church, but I am afraid we have settled for talent.

Sometimes I hear people use the word *talents* when they are talking about spiritual gifts. It is easy to confuse the two. I like to define the difference this way: talent is an endowment from God, while spiritual gifting is an empowerment of God. Talent comes from our human genetics. Spiritual gifting comes from our divine genetics. Human talent is natural, but gifting is spiritual (1 Corinthians 2:14–16 NKJV). Because it is so easy to confuse the two, we have filled our church leadership positions with talented people who may have phenomenal personalities but who, in many cases, lack character. They may have incredible abilities but no anointing. Doing for them is more important than being. Work becomes more important than worship.

Actually, there is no such thing as being too busy: It is a matter of misplaced priorities. It is possible to become so active that we do not know the difference between a busy life and a full life. We continue eating the tainted fruit that comes from substituting what God has given to his body—the church—for what is expedient, and we keep getting sicker.

God gives spiritual gifts to people for the purpose of building (edifying), exhorting (encouraging), and comforting (encouraging) his body—the church. Since talent is an endowment from God and not an empowerment of God, talent in and of itself cannot provide the body with what it needs to be healthy and vibrant; especially in this last season.

God gives spiritual gifts (supernatural abilities), to each of his children for the benefit of others. Your spiritual gift(s) is not for you. It has been given to you for the benefit of the entire body of Christ. A fruit tree does not eat its own fruit. The fruit of the tree is for others. The body can grow and remain healthy as we eat the fruit from one another's tree. This is why we do the community of faith a disservice by withdrawing from assembling. It is denying our brothers and sisters what they need for their spiritual nourishment.

Most individuals within the body of Christ have no idea what their spiritual gifts are. Far too many Christians are not even sure if God still gives spiritual gifts to his children. This combination of not knowing what our spiritual gifts are, and not being convinced that spiritual gifts are still available, has substantially weakened the body of Christ and has made us ineffective in most places. Most local churches are no stronger or more effective than the local civic clubs. The lion's share of churches can close their buildings today, and most communities would never know it. Their existence has had no effect whatsoever on their community. This is the only outcome when we substitute talent for spiritual gifting.

POSITIVE THINKING OVER FAITH

Once the church accepts talent over gifting, it makes it so much easier to fall away from faith and embrace positive thinking. The word of God does not say that without positive thinking it is impossible to please God. It says that without faith it is impossible to please God (Hebrew 11:6 NKJV). Is positive thinking important? It certainly is, but not at the expense of the word of God. I do my best to surround myself with people who have optimistic attitudes about life. We need all the positive influence that we can possibly get. I also know that having a great attitude can only take you so far.

We are increasingly hearing messages preached from pulpits today that are more motivational speeches than they are messages from the word of God. I read something not long ago that tripped my trigger. "When a preacher becomes a motivational speaker, the congregation becomes happy sinners" (John Wesley). I have some sad news for you. We are filling buildings all around the world with happy sinners.

Jesus said that if we make ourselves at home in the word of God, we will know the truth, and the truth we know will set us free (John 8:31–32 NKJV). A positive speech may rally the troops, but it will not equip the troops for battle. Positive thinking speeches will turn the church into a cruise ship filled with contented sinners, when it should be a battleship filled with courageous Saints. In this last season, the church must be what God has intended for it to be; a warship that even the gates of hell cannot stop.

The fruit of faith will be a positive attitude. I have never met a believer strong in their faith who has not been a positive person. How can we not be positive when we have placed our faith in a God who has no beginning or end; a God who knows everything about everything, who can do all things, and who can be everywhere at the same time? Our God has promised that he will never leave or forsake us (Hebrews 13:5 NKJV). His heart is always toward us. That means that if he loved me yesterday when I was lovable, he will love me today when I am unlovable. How good is that? "Jesus Christ is the same yesterday, today, and forever" (Hebrews 13:8 NKJV). He is immutable.

Positive thinking is a person's attempt to stay positive while living in a negative world. We have been convinced that if we can keep a positive attitude (focusing on the good in all situations) long enough, one day things will change. But they never do because they cannot. Jesus told us, "These things I have spoken to you, that *in Me you may have peace. In the world you will have tribulation*; but be of good cheer, I have overcome the world" (John 16:33 NKJV; emphasis added). Peace comes from being in Christ by faith, not from being in the world with a positive attitude.

Faith, on the other hand, is not a struggle to stay positive; it is living in the reality of the revealed word of God. "Faith is the confidence that what we hope for will actually happen; it gives us assurance about things we cannot see" (Hebrews 11:1 NLT). Here's an acrostic for faith you may want to file in your memory bank. Faith is: **F**orgetting **A**ll, **I** **T**rust **H**im.

In many churches today, faith has been taken off the menu and replaced by positive thinking. And we wonder why we are not seeing the Spirit of God move in power in our midst.

MAN'S OPINION OVER GOD'S WORD

When positive thinking replaces faith, man's opinion will become more important to people than the word of God. What we are left with is a full-blown spiritual COVID syndrome.

The symptoms of spiritual COVID start with what appears to be something benign: doing. There is absolutely nothing wrong with working hard; it is an admirable quality. But when doing takes precedence over being, human ability will be deemed more credible than divine anointing. Our doing (work) should flow out of our being—our new creation identities. Once human ability becomes a priority, personality will be what attracts our attention. We certainly want and need the right person, so we search for an individual who has the personality that we feel will get the job done. We are usually not content (unknowingly) to wait and see if our person of choice has character. This is why so many on our leadership teams turn out to be characters who are lacking in character.

Since our focus is on personality, we are easily drawn to a person's talent. Having the right personality and possessing talent is an unbeatable combination—we think. Spiritual gifting is not that high on our list. It is not because we think spiritual gifting is not important; it just does not cross our minds. Since it is not on our minds, it does not make our list of must-haves. A person needs to be selected because of who he or she is, not for what the individual has the potential to become.

This entire process of moving from one symptom to the next is not a cascade; it is a slow trickle. Because the church has not been on its toes, positive thinking has wormed its way into the church and replaced faith in many places. Once this happens, the next stage is for man's opinion to take precedence over the scriptures.

In many pulpits today, man's opinion is being expressed and embraced over the word of God. When you hear someone promoting and accepting what God has condemned, you are hearing someone's opinion. I am amazed at how much I am hearing today that is alien to the word of God. I pray that I never reach the point when I am not shocked when man's opinion usurps the word of God. "Fools have no interest in understanding; they only want to air their own opinions" (Proverbs 18:2 NLT).

In many places we have embraced man's opinion even when it is incongruent with the word of God. We cannot accept what God says is wrong and expect God to bless it. If it was wrong when God said it, it is still wrong today, and it will not become right just because someone says it is or if we pass laws legalizing it. It is not the *will* of God if it goes against the *word* of God.

We do not need to defend the word of God. We just need to preach the word; it will defend itself. It was C. H. Spurgeon who said, "Defend the Bible? I would as soon defend a lion! Unchain it and it will defend itself." Case closed!

A person's opinion will always be in a state of flux, but the word of God will not, because God's word is absolute truth. Absolute truth is something that is always true. Absolute truth is always true no matter what the circumstances may be. God's truth is not subject to man's opinion. Truth cannot be changed. This is why it is called *truth*. The word of God is infallible, unalterable, and the unadulterated truth. God's word is eternal; therefore, it will never change. "All scripture is inspired by God and is useful to teach us what is true and to make us realize what is wrong in our lives It corrects us when we are wrong and teaches us to do what is right. God uses it to prepare and equip his people to do every good work" (2 Timothy 3:16–17 NLT). If God's word is not absolute truth, then what we stand on today may not support us tomorrow.

A GLIMPSE OF
THE LAST-SEASON
CHURCH

I want to begin this chapter by asking a shocking question. Have we become so proficient at "doing church" that we really don't need God's help? I am convinced that this is not something we really believe; it is something we do without thinking. We have become so techie and so savvy at putting on productions that we have convinced ourselves that bigger and brighter is always better. This is why we keep building larger buildings, buying more land, and adding satellite campuses. The bigger our facilities are, the more people we can gather. It is not hard to attract a large crowd today, but whatever you do to get them, you must increase what you are doing to keep them. The worship performance must get bigger and grander. The church has been eating the fruit of what this has produced for many years now, and it has made the body (church) sick.

A large number of people come to church buildings on a weekly basis and are convinced that because they are faithful to come, they are a part of the true church. There is a big difference between being a guest in the house and a family member of the house. It is possible to be an attachment to the body of Christ and not be a part of the body of Christ: much like a watch or a ring is an attachment to our physical bodies but not a part of our bodies. When the body hurts or is injured, the watch and ring does not feel a thing—only being an attachment.

In the introduction of this book, I made a statement that I hope caused you to pause and think. I said that every church is not the Lord's church, but the Lord has his church in every church. I have said this for many years now, but it is more relevant today than ever before. For years, our church buildings have been filled with Jesus fans, worship fans, pulpit personality fans, Bible study fans, ministry fans, and the list goes on. But there is a stark difference between a team player and a team fan. A team player is the one who wears the uniform and participates. Team players are the ones who have skin in the game. A fan may wear a team jersey and a hat but has absolutely no investment in the game. A player is a participator, but a fan is a spectator. Fans can be very capricious, too. They have the propensity to boo their team if they are not performing up to their potential or to the fan's expectations. Some even call for the resignation of the coach if there are more Ls in the loss column than Ws in the win column. Fans can be hard to please and may even be open to shop for a new team if things are not going as they think they should. Most fans think they know more about the game than the coach or the players.

I would wager that you know I am not talking about a sports team. This is the modern-day church I am describing. Pew sitters have no skin in the game because they are spectators and not participators. They may wear their worship jerseys, preaching jerseys, Bible study jerseys, or ministry hat, but they have no dog in the fight. They will certainly make their voices heard and give their opinions when things are not going the way they think they should. They may even call for a change in the coaching staff. A fan will be content to spectate but has no desire to get involved. These days are coming to an end.

In January 2007, the Lord gave me a glimpse of what the church will look and act like when the time is right. A pastor friend of mine, Dorman Duggan, and his dear wife, Jani, put together a team consisting of twenty-three people for a ten-day mission trip to Uganda, which is in the central part of Africa. I don't think those who went on this trip had any idea how much this experience was going to transform their lives—forever.

While we were away, a lady by the name of Irene Hughes was praying specifically for each member of our team. Her husband, Fred, was an integral part of this mission effort. As the Lord revealed specific things to her about an individual team member, she would write it down. We all knew that Irene was praying for us, but we did not know she was asking the Holy Spirit to show her what each person needed to experience on this trip.

After returning home, we had a homecoming gathering so we could share our experiences and reminisce about the special moments we had in Uganda. This is when Irene gave each person a written copy of what she felt the Lord had given her concerning them during our time away. Here is what she received from the Lord about me. ["Wayne] You will be convinced that the word works." She said several other things that were spot-on, but this one statement is what was so meaningful to me. I would be convinced, completely persuaded, that the word of God is true, and that God's word can be trusted. My experience in Uganda changed everything for me. When I received the vision about the controlled burn, the Holy Spirit took me back to 2007 and the experience we had in Uganda. I saw what the Lord's church will look and act like in this last season. God is bringing his church out of intubation. I am convinced that we will experience the very things we saw and participated in when we were in Uganda. It will not be something that happens occasionally; it will become the lifestyle of the true church in this last season. This is why there must be a controlled burn. All the stuff and fluff that is getting in the way must be taken out. The Lord had to intubate his church so he could get her healthy and ready for this last-season assignment.

A GLIMPSE OF THE LAST-SEASON CHURCH

To make sure that I have given an honest and truthful testimony, I gave what you are about to read to several people who were a part of our Ugandan team to proofread. I do not want to exaggerate the story or embellish our experience in Uganda in any form or fashion. If anything, I have pulled back on the reins a little.

Upon arriving in Kampala, Uganda, we were taken by van to a town sixty miles away called Mityana. This sixty-mile trip took approximately four hours. To say the roads were a little less than desirable would be an understatement. There's only one road that I've traveled in my lifetime that was worse. It was a thirty-mile stretch of road in Kenya.

Our typical day in Mityana looked something like this. Every morning around nine o'clock we would arrive at a building where twenty-five hundred-plus people had gathered to worship and hear the word of God taught. Most of those in attendance were pastors and leaders of churches. A large percentage of them had traveled miles to attend this meeting; some came from neighboring countries. Because they had very little money, and there were limited places for them to stay, they slept on the ground around the building. By the time we got to the meeting every morning, they had already been worshipping for several hours. To say they were hungry for God would be an understatement.

The team would teach and minister the word of God until 2:00 or 2:30 p.m., nonstop. After that we would go to where we were staying, have something to eat, clean up, and around 5:00 p.m. we would head out for the area where we were holding the crusade. When we left the meeting to prepare for the evening service, the people kept worshipping and interceding in prayer. The crusade was held in an open space that could accommodate thirty to forty thousand people. Nightly services were held for six straight days. On Sunday, we went out in teams of two to local churches to minister. Some teams traveled to churches that were several hours away.

The stage where the worshippers stood, and where we preached the word from was approximately forty feet long and twelve feet wide. This makeshift stage had a huge swag in the middle of it. Our team took bets on what night the stage would collapse. Because it was so flimsy, we believed there was no way it could survive the week. It did sag considerably, but to our utter amazement, it never collapsed. That was a miracle, too, because Ugandan worshippers are very active, and aggressive choreography is an integral part of their worship.

Every night of the crusade the Holy Spirit led us to follow a specific sequence of ministry. The first thing the team did was present a message of salvation. The burning compassion in our hearts was to give everyone attending an opportunity to accept Jesus Christ as their Lord and Savior. We wanted to make sure that we presented a clear message of how an individual can have a new birth experience with Christ. At the conclusion of the message, people were given the opportunity to accept and receive the new creation life that can only be found in Jesus Christ. Each message was well received, and people responded by the hundreds.

After the salvation invitation, we would immediately go into healing ministry. An appeal was made to those who needed a healing touch from the Lord. Again, the response was incredible. People came en masse to be touched by God. We saw several children who had problems with their vision or who could not see at all regain their sight. Others who could not hear began to hear—some for the first time. We saw people who were lame and infirm made whole; hundreds of people suffering from fever were healed. It was a magnificent sight to behold.

Then came the chaos. We began the deliverance ministry. I cannot adequately describe the chaos and demonic turbulence this created. To say the demonic realm was stirred up would be an understatement. The kingdom of darkness rose and tried everything to discourage us and to get us to back off. The first night I was so overwhelmed with what was going on that I had thoughts of running. Oh, yes, I did. Then it hit me. Where will I run to? I am in Africa, for crying out loud. It is not like I can run home and hide under my bed. It came down to fight or flight. My options were limited, so I decided to take the "l" out of flight.

The first three days were borderline runaways. On Thursday night of the crusade, peace swept over the entire area, and the demonic realm was afraid to raise its head. The intimidator was now intimidated. Each night more and more people would come to receive Christ, to be healed and set free. We saw several children and adults receive their eyesight and have their hearing restored. Untold numbers of people were healed of fever. Lame people who were touched by the hand of God began to leap and dance in joy. We witnessed those who had been driven to the edge of insanity by demonic forces freed and healed. This boy (me) from a Baptist background prayed for a woman whose head was the size of a large grapefruit. She was hissing like a serpent. I was careful to keep her chin in the palm of my hand so she could not bite me. Her tongue was flickering in and out just like a snake. When it was all over, she was healed and set free. Her head had returned to its normal size, and she danced in joy as she praised the Lord. You could see the glory of God all over her. The look on my interpreter's face was priceless. Seeing this woman set free from demonic possession inspired him so much that he started grabbing people so he could pray for them. When the Spirit moves, it is contagious.

One of my spiritual sons and I were praying for a lady who looked like she was a hundred-years old. Her right leg was turned completely backwards and locked and was as hard as a rock. As we laid our hands on her and prayed, Brett yelled out, "Pastor, feel this!" You could feel her leg rotating back into its proper place. Once this happened, she jumped to her feet and began to dance and praise the Lord like a young girl. Those in front of the crowd who could see what was going on went wild. These people knew one another. They were aware of everyone's physical condition because they lived in the same village together for years. Every time someone was healed and set free, people would start passing individuals over their shoulders and stacking them at our feet like cordwood in front of the sagging stage. Our entire team was literally stepping on people as we ministered.

All twenty-three members of the team were engaged. You could hear screams, growls, hisses, and all kinds of demonic manifestations. Demonic people in the crowd did everything imaginable to disrupt, intimidate, and hinder what we were doing. I was so proud of our team. Not one team member backed up, backed off, or became passive. Everyone was a participator. The church was doing what it is designed to do—destroy the works of the enemy. This was the schedule we followed for six days—Monday through Saturday.

When we did deliverance ministry on Thursday night, there was an incredible peace present. A holy hush was over the entire area. The sweet presence of God was tangible. My pastor friend Dorman Duggan said, "It was like we were inside a huge bubble, protected and impervious to what was going on around us."

Let me remind you again of the word God had given to Irene Hughes for me. I would be convinced that God's word works. For the first twenty-seven years of my ministry, I pastored a Southern Baptist Church. During those years, I heard and read about supernatural manifestations of God being poured out, but I never had a firsthand experience. For the last twenty-three years, I have pastored a nondenominational church and have been exposed to some exciting moves of the Spirit but not on the scale of what took place in Africa. When the Spirit of God began to move in power and demonstration, this was one bug-eyed Baptist boy seeing firsthand what he had heard about and always wanted to see but was not absolutely convinced he would ever see it. Well, this dude came back from Uganda a believer. I really believe my Baptist grounding, especially in the word, prepared me for where I am today. I would not trade for either.

One night during the crusade, I was standing next to Brett (the young man who had prayed with me for the lady with the twisted and petrified leg) and one of the local pastors. This man of God had one of those "what in the world" is happening looks on his face. He leaned over and whispered in Brett McGraw's ear, "We have never seen anything like this before." Brett responded, "We haven't either." These local pastors assumed that what was taking place at the crusade was common to us. They had no clue that we were just as astonished and amazed as they were at what was happening. We were learning that the word of God works! God was showing us what the church would look like and what the church will be doing during this last season.

This last-day season the true church has entered is not for a specific group that identifies itself with a sign or a denominational brand. This season is for the body of Christ—God's true church. What we saw and experienced in Uganda will be what the last-season church looks like and experiences every day, twenty-four seven. God is raising his church out of every church. The Lord's church is coming out of intubation.

I am not finished with my Uganda testimony. I will share more of this experience with you in the next chapter and in chapter 6.

A NEW NORMAL—FOR THE TRUE CHURCH

Our experience in Uganda sounds abnormal to the normal Christian. I cannot tell you how many times I have shared this story, whether it be in a small Bible study group or in a large church meeting and have gotten that "get-out-of-my-face" stare. I feel that most honest believers want to believe that things like this do happen, but it is so far outside of our normal Christian experience. When you try to understand the supernatural with the natural mind, you are left bemused. It is like trying to make sense when there is no sense. What you end up with is nonsense.

Not long after we returned from Africa, I went to visit my mother. She knew where I had been and was curious to hear what

I had to say about our trip. I will never forget the look on her face as she sat quietly and listened to me share our incredible experience in Uganda. Several times I noticed tears pooling in the corner of her eyes. I went into greater detail about the things we saw and experienced than I have shared in this chapter. When I finished telling my mother what we saw God do in Uganda, she sat there and stared at me in a loving way. When she finally spoke, these are the words that came out of her mouth: "I don't think you should tell your brother and sister what you just told me."

What do you think my mother meant by that? The only way for us to really know is for her to tell us. Since my beautiful mother is now in the presence of the Lord, we must wait for her answer. Here is my interpretation of what she meant. "Son, if you tell people what you just told me, they may think you have lost your mind and that you have gotten off your meds. People may think you are one of those religious fanatics who have become so heavenly minded they are of no earthly good. I'm your mother, and because I love you, I will keep what you told me to myself, and I would encourage you to do the same."

My precious mother was not being mean or rude to me. She loved her son to a fault. I was not shocked that she responded this way either. She did not want her son to look like a spiritual weirdo. What will people think when they hear stories like this? What she did not know was that I had already shared (in detail) what we experienced in Uganda with my brother, Keith. It got his spiritual juices flowing, and he was ready to pack his bags and head to Uganda.

Leonard Ravenhill exposed the truth about what Christianity looks like today when he said, "Christianity today is so subnormal that if any Christian began to act like a normal New Testament Christian, he would be considered abnormal." I would say it this way: "Most believers are so subnormal that if they ever got normal, they would appear abnormal." If you have ever been around a Christian who appears to be abnormal, what might that be saying about you?

A year or so after our trip to Uganda, we had Pastor Robert Mponye as our guest here in the States. Pastor Robert is a local pastor in Mityana, Uganda, who was responsible for the logistics of the entire crusade that we held in his hometown. During one of our meetings with Pastor Robert, we had a Q&A session to give our people the opportunity to hear his side of the story. One of our dear ladies (a retired schoolteacher) was one of the first to speak. "Pastor Robert, our pastor has told us some incredible stories about what happened when they were in your country. We know he would not tell us something that was not true, but ..." Having been in the ministry for fifty years, I have heard the conjunction *but* used many times. I know that what follows the *but* is what a person really believes. "I know our pastor would not tell us something that was not true, *but*—we would like to hear what you have to say about it." You could hear a pin drop as Pastor Robert began to recount what took place during our time in Uganda. "Everything you've heard your pastor say is the unadulterated truth. The people who received healing and deliverance are still healed and free. The people who accepted and received Jesus Christ as their Lord and Savior are engaged and active with local churches in our community. Because of that special moment in time, we will never be the same."

The follow-up question for Pastor Robert was, "Why do these things happen in your country, and we don't see them happen here in our country?" Pastor Robert did not hesitate with his reply. "You have options." In other words, here in America we have access to things that the people in Uganda do not have. Christ is their only hope. We have options. For a long time when I shared this story, I would emphasize the part about us having options to justify why we do not see God move like we saw him move in Uganda. One day the Holy Spirit began to nudge me away from that conclusion. The reason we do not see movements of God like we saw in Uganda is because we do not expect them to happen, or we do not believe they will happen. It has very little to do with having options. If we believe that having options is why we do not see God move like we did in Uganda, we shift the blame for our unbelief to something over which we have no control. It justifies our unbelief. Having options or not having options does not inhibit God from doing mighty works among us. This sounds like the blame game that was played in Genesis. Adam blamed Eve for his disobedience, and he also blamed God: "This woman You gave me" (Genesis 3:12 NKJV). It's her fault God, and remember, you are the one who gave her to me. Eve blamed the serpent for her rebellion. Having options may have a small part in us not seeing God move like we saw him move in Uganda, but it is not the primary reason. We have become comfortable in our subnormal spiritual condition. When Christians begin to act normal, they will appear as being abnormal to those who are subnormal.

Things are changing and changing rapidly. The church is rising in this last season. The controlled burn that we have been going through is exposing what has been there all the time. People have grown tired of the status quo. Many are thinking, "There has got to be more than what we are experiencing." We have learned how to do church well, but in this season, it is time for us to be the church. We may have reached the point where we think we do not need God to do church, but we certainly need God to be the church.

The discussion about the exodus of our young people from the church has been going on for a while. I have heard all kinds of reasons why it is hard to keep young people hooked up with the church today. Some of the reasons given have merit. We even have conferences that deal with this phenomenon. Here is my take on why so many older teenagers and young adults no longer have a desire to be a part of the local church today. We do not lose them when they get older; we lose them when they are children, and they leave when they get old enough to make that decision. If our young people could experience the power of God and participate in a move of his Spirit, they would be running to be a part of the local body of Christ—not from it. This will be the new normal for the church in this last season. The controlled burn is not over.

A few years ago, I shared with one of our Life Groups what I feel this last season will look like for the church. People will be knocking on our doors seeking answers on how to survive during difficult times. They will not be interested in hearing you tell them about the journeys of Paul or be overly concerned about your doctrine and theological position on anything. Being able to quote all sixty-six books of the Bible will not impress them either. Their interest will not be in what programs your church has to offer. They need to hear and see the power and presence of the Holy Spirit because they no longer have options. It is Christ or nothing. If that knock comes to your door, what do you have to give them? I do not think people will be searching out those who appear normal in their Christian faith. I am convinced they will be looking for the ones who appear abnormal.

I talk to pastors on a regular basis who are convinced there will be a resurgence of small home church groups. I am certainly not implying the end is coming for large or megachurches. We are blessed to have some incredible churches that are very large and are doing great things to expand the kingdom of God, not only here in America but around the world. I am certainly not anti-megachurch. But what I do see is an interest and a desire to rediscover the New Testament paradigm of the home church that we read about in the book of Acts. In later chapters, I will talk about the advantages these small home churches will have over large gatherings and their contribution to the survival of believers in this last season. I am convinced that the small home church groups will draw most of those who God is bringing out of intubation in this last season.

I spent several years pastoring in a specific area of my state where a person's position on eschatology was high on the list of criteria for them to be given the right hand of fellowship. To not hold a certain position was to be labeled a heretic. Thank goodness most of that no longer exists. We may have different opinions about eschatology, but one thing we all can agree on is that Christ is coming back because he said he would. Peter talks about how we as the church need to conduct ourselves considering that we are living in the last days.

[Now] The end of the world is coming soon. Therefore, be earnest and disciplined in your prayers. Most important of all, continue to show deep love for each other, for love covers a multitude of sins. Cheerfully share your home with those who need a meal or a place to stay. God has given each of you a gift from his great variety of spiritual gifts. Use them well to serve one another. Do you have the gift of speaking? Then speak as though God himself were speaking through you. Do you have the gift of helping others? Do it with all the strength and energy that God supplies. Then everything you do will bring glory to God through Jesus Christ. All glory and power to him forever and ever! Amen." (1 Peter 4:7–11 NLT)

Whatever we do in this last season, let's do it for the glory of God and for the good of one another.

When will the Lord return? No one knows. I would encourage you to be leery of anyone who says they do know. We do know he is coming again because he promised he would. Until then, let's live as if Christ died yesterday, arose today, and is coming back tomorrow. I read an interesting post the other day that said, "I am no longer looking for the signs of the time, I'm listening for the sound of the trumpet" (source unknown).

Let me conclude this chapter by answering the question I began with. Have we become so proficient at "doing church" that we really do not need God's help? I am convinced this is not something we think; it is something we do without thinking. The church is filled with a plethora of talent and technology that makes it so easy to create an atmosphere that will attract a crowd, but are we attracting the presence of the Holy Spirit? Since Christ is our life, we can't do anything without him (Colossians 3:4 NKJV).

A SEASON OF
EXPECTATION

What about the options I referred to in the last chapter? Are the options we are blessed with keeping us from experiencing a move of the Spirit of God like we saw in Uganda? At one time I would have said yes. When we get sick, we have access to incredible health care. That becomes our first option, so praying for healing is usually low on our list. We do pray for healing, but it's usually after we have seen our personal health-care provider. People from all over the world come to America seeking health care because we have the best there is to offer.

When we face a financial crisis, we have access to financial institutions that can step in and lend a helping hand. We do have options. But having options is not what keeps us from seeing and experiencing what we saw in Uganda. Our problem is that we do not believe or expect miracles, signs, and wonders to happen here. We have a lack-of-faith pandemic that is infecting and affecting the church today. And it has gone undiagnosed for a while now.

What if things change? What if our options become less and less or are even taken away? What if health care becomes limited and restricted because of one's health condition, age, political affiliation, where they live, ad infinitum? What will you do if we reach the tipping point where health care is rationed or becomes unavailable?

I am afraid we may be approaching what I call a Samson moment. Even though Samson had God's anointing on his life for the purpose of delivering Israel from the hand of the Philistines, he thought he could flirt with sin and not be contaminated by it. One day he was lulled to sleep in the lap of Delilah. While he slept, she was able to do what no one had been able to accomplish. Delilah was able to nullify his strength by cutting his hair. Samson was a Nazarite by birth, and one thing a Nazirite could not do was cut his hair. When Samson awoke from his sleep he said, "I will go out as before, at other times, and shake myself free! *But he did not know that the Lord had departed from him*" (Judges 16:20 NKJV; emphasis added). The last words of this verse may be the saddest words in the entire Bible: "He did not know the Lord had departed from him." This could be the epitaph of the institutional church: They do not know the presence of the Lord has departed.

THIS LAST SEASON IS A SEASON OF EXPECTATION

This last season that I believe the church has entered will be a season of expectation. Not only are we believing there will be an incredible move of God in our midst; we are expecting God to move among us in power and in glory.

Let me take you back to the preparation stages for our Ugandan experience. It may help you to better understand why we had the experiences we had. After accepting pastor Robert Mponye's invitation to come to Uganda to teach pastors and church leaders during the day and to lead a crusade at night, my pastor friend Dorman Duggan explained to him how we would conduct the nightly crusades, especially the order of the services, and why. I covered that in the last chapter. It was the preparation stage that laid the groundwork for our expectations of what we would personally experience in Uganda.

Let me begin by reminding you of the answer Pastor Robert gave when he was asked the question "Why does this happen in your country but not here?" He said three words: you have options. After thinking about his answer for several years, the Holy Spirit began to give me revelation into why some see these incredible moves of God and others don't. Why were we able to have this experience in Uganda but not in one of our Sunday services here in America? Was it because the people we were ministering to had no options? For years I would have said options are the reason. When I started receiving the revelation about this last season I feel we have just entered, I began to see something I had never seen before. We can take options out of the equation. We had this incredible experience in Uganda because we believed it would happen, and we expected it to happen.

When the initial plans were being made for our trip to Africa, we had meetings to talk about logistics. During these meetings someone would share something he or she had read or shared a story someone told about incredible moves of God in the continent of Africa. Every story we heard increased our expectations. By the time we boarded our flight to Uganda, our expectations for what we were going to experience were sky high. Every person on our team not only believed we would see the glory of God; we all expected to see miracles, signs, and wonders.

Unbeknown to us, the same thing was happening in Africa. Pastor Robert Mponye was sharing with his team what we were going to do when we got there. Even though they had agreed that we could do deliverance during the crusade, they admitted they knew nothing about deliverance ministry. They assumed it was standard operating procedure for us here in America. Let me insert an addendum here: deliverance ministry should be standard operating procedure for the church here in American, but I'm afraid it is not. We falsely assume that deliverance ministry is something that you do in third world countries, but it is not needed in our sophisticated society. The unvarnished truth is that we need it just as much as they do in Africa—maybe even more.

Back to our story. The Ugandan leadership team was now thinking like our American team. They began to not only believe they would see miracles, signs, and wonders; they expected to see them. Both sides believed and expected the miraculous to happen. We were in agreement of expectancy now, and neither side was aware of it. It was not about having options or not having options. It was about believing and expecting God to do great things.

THE CHURCH OF ACTS 12

I cannot tell you how many times in my fifty years of ministry that I have heard these words: "We need to look and act like the early church." I have a news flash for you, beloved; in many ways we do. All we must do is take a close look at the church in Acts 12.

When King Herod Agrippa saw how pleased the Jewish people were over him persecuting some of the believers in the church, he stepped up his assault. He had James, the brother of John, killed with the sword. Peter had been arrested and placed in prison. Herod's intent was to bring Peter out of prison for a public trial after Passover and have him killed. Herod was intent on decimating the early church by eliminating the leadership. Speaking of the church, where is the church when all of this is going on?

The church was gathered in the home of Mary, the mother of John Mark, to pray for Peter's safety and deliverance. This is encouraging: the church is doing what you would assume it would be doing at a time like this—praying. "Peter was therefore kept in prison, but constant prayer was offered to God for him *by the church*" (Acts 12:5 NKJV; emphasis added).

Suddenly, an angel of God appears by Peter's side and wakes him up. The chains that had Peter fastened to two soldiers fell off when he opened his eyes. "Then the angel said to him, 'Gird yourself and tie on your sandals,' and so he did. And he said to him, 'Put on your garment and follow me'" (Acts 12:8 NKJV). The prayers of the church are getting through. These mighty prayer warriors are praying down heaven. No wonder people say that we should look and act like the early church. Not too fast; the whole story has not been told yet.

The angel takes Peter past the first and second guard posts, then to the locked iron gate leading into the city. Right before Peter's eyes, the locked iron gate opens of its own accord. Once outside the prison walls, the angel departs, and Peter is left alone. At first Peter thinks he is having a vision. When he regains his wits, he realizes the Lord had sent an angel to deliver him from the hand of Herod and the expectations of the Jewish people who wanted to see him executed. The prayers of the church have been answered.

"So when he (Peter) had considered this, he came to the house of Mary, the mother of John whose surname was Mark, where *many were gathered together praying*" (Acts 12:12 NKJV; emphasis added). Can you imagine the excitement and rejoicing that is going to take place when the church sees their prayers have been answered? Heaven has just kissed earth with a miracle because of the prayers of a believing and expecting church.

Peter makes his way to the home of Mary where the church is engaged in intercessory prayer. "And as Peter knocked at the door of the gate, a girl named Rhoda came to answer" (Acts 12:13 NKJV). When she recognized Peter's voice, she was overwhelmed with excitement. Instead of opening the door to let him in, she ran back inside and told everyone that Peter was standing at the gate. You would expect everyone to jump to their feet and run to welcome Peter. Their prayers have been answered. It's time to celebrate. This was not their response. This was: "But they said to her, 'You are beside yourself'" (Acts 12:15 NKJV). In other words, you have lost your mind, young lady; Peter is in prison.

But she kept insisting that Peter was at the front gate. Those praying for a miracle still did not believe Peter had been freed. "It is his angel," they said (Acts 12:15 NKJV). The prayers of the church must have sounded something like this: "God, we ask for your divine intervention. Set Peter free. God rest his soul." "Lord, you can do all things. We are believing you for a miracle. We are going to miss ole Peter. He was such a great guy." The people (church) did not believe that God would answer their prayers. Maybe we do look and act like the early church.

Peter kept knocking on the door of the gate. Finally, they opened the door and saw Peter standing, unchained and free before their very eyes. Their prayers had been answered, but they were greatly surprised (Acts 12:16 NKJV). I would say the church of today looks and acts much like the early church. It amazes us when our prayers are answered, when the opposite should be true. We should be astonished when our prayers are not answered.

Isn't it amazing that most of us are stunned when our prayers are answered? Could the reason be because we (church) don't believe or expect our prayers will be answered? This unbelief and lack of expectation has created an environment that has greatly weakened the effectiveness of the church today. For the most part, prayer has become as exciting as changing a flat tire. It's not much fun, but it must be done.

A lack of faith and expectation creates an environment where we don't see many miracles. Unbelief and a lack of expectation on the part of the church has created an atmosphere where God can't work. This is why we don't see more of the inexplicable happening in our church services than we do. Listen to how Matthew describes Jesus's visit to his hometown of Nazareth: "And so he did only a few miracles there *because of their unbelief*" (Matthew 13:58 NLT; emphasis added). Have we created an atmosphere where God cannot work? Leading up to this last season, the church has become so predictable (we don't expect anything to happen) and so comfortable (we're satisfied with nothing happening) that our expectations of experiencing the supernatural are pegged on zero.

A lack of faith and expectation creates an environment where people are not delivered. We can go weeks, months, and even years and not see people delivered and set free from what has them bound. People come to our church services week in and week out bound by the chains of addiction, rejection, hurt, guilt, hopelessness, grudges, bitterness, and self-condemnation, and they leave the same way they came. This is not the church of this last season.

A lack of faith and expectation creates an environment where prayers are not answered. Instead of being amazed when they are, we should be beside ourselves when they are not. Because we don't see more of the miraculous when we pray, it creates more doubt and lessens our expectations to see our prayers answered. If you don't believe anything will happen, you will not be disappointed. "Blessed is he who expects nothing, for he shall never be disappointed" (Alexander Pope).

A lack of faith and expectation creates an environment where the church is never awed. When was the last time you left a worship service in a state of reverential awe? You can always tell when there has been a move of the Spirit of God in a service because the people do not want to leave. When God manifests his presence, you don't want to leave it. All you want to do is bask in the moment and sit at his feet. Nothing, and I mean absolutely nothing, can compare to the sweet presence of the Lord. He is our life (Colossians 3:4 NKJV).

A lack of faith and expectation creates an environment where the world is never disturbed. If the church is never awed by what God is doing, I assure you, the world will never feel uncomfortable with what the church is doing. And it should be troubled every time the church comes together. The kingdom of light should always make the kingdom of darkness uneasy. How was the world disturbed when Peter was miraculously delivered from prison? "At dawn *there was a great commotion* among the soldiers about what had happened to Peter. Herod Agrippa ordered a thorough search for him. When he couldn't be found, Herod interrogated the guards and sentenced them to death" (Acts 12:18–19 NLT; emphasis added). It was not a good day to be a prison guard in King Herod's prison system.

Not long after this, Herod died from a sickness. Here is his biblical epitaph: "[So] he was consumed with worms and died" (Acts 12:23 NLT). Herod became worm food while the word of God continued to spread, and there were many new believers (Acts 12:24 NLT).

RIOTS—REVIVAL—OR COVERED-DISH SUPPERS

I think it was N. T. Wright who said, "Wherever St. Paul went, there was a riot. Wherever I go, they serve tea." Here is my spin on it: "Wherever Paul went, there was a riot or a revival. Wherever I go, they serve covered-dish suppers." Have you noticed that church dinners are better attended than prayer meetings? Concerts draw bigger crowds than regular church services. Why is that? Could it be because we hunger more for physical food than we do spiritual food? Is it possible we would rather be entertained by a talented group of singers than worship our heavenly Father? Maybe we don't see more riots or revivals because we operate on an empty stomach and not a full heart. It's a sad day when a growling stomach will get more attention than a groaning spirit.

The church has become so predictable and comfortable that if we entertain thoughts of doing things differently, the response is usually hostile. When things are predictable, people can expect what will or will not happen, and they like that. There will usually be an agreeable spirit among the people as long as things stay comfortable. Whatever you do, don't disturb people's comfort zones. People have gotten comfortable with their comfort.

The Holy Spirit will do just that: He will draw you out of your comfort zone. Let me remind you of something I said in the introduction about our comfort zones. For those of us who want to participate in this last-season move of the church, we must be willing to give up some things that we have found comfort in. God will take us out of our comfort zones into a new zone where he is our only comfort. God is into new. He never adds new to the old, nor does he mix or blend the old with the new. "And the one sitting on the throne said, 'Look, I am making everything new!'" (Revelation 21:5 NLT).

EXPECTATION IS THE SEEDBED FOR MIRACLES

Our church buildings are filled with people who have come with little or no expectations whatsoever that anything out of the normal will happen. They have come because that's what Christians do—they attend church. They come, they leave, they come back, they leave—the religious merry-go-round continues. Most people who attend church are not expecting anything to take place other than what they have experienced before.

Faith and expectation are not the same thing. It is possible to have faith but not have expectation, but you can't have expectation without having faith. Have you noticed that it is much easier to believe for the healing of others than it is to believe for your own? I have no problem praying and believing for someone's healing. I have laid my hands on and prayed for many people and have seen them recover. In some cases, like in Uganda, I have witnessed miraculous healings. The healings were instantaneous. It is often a different story when it comes to me. I certainly believe that God heals today. I have no doubts about that. But sometimes I find myself not expecting him to heal me. It is possible to have faith without having expectation, but you cannot have expectation without having faith. Faith comes before expectation.

Expectation is the seedbed for miracles to happen. If there is anything conspicuous by its absence in the church today, it is expectation. We did not see anything happen out of the ordinary last week when we came to church, so why should we expect anything unusual to happen this week? We could take this even further: Since we did not see anything out of the ordinary happen last year, why should we expect anything different this year? The mundane and the predictable continue.

Let me give you a fresh testimony of faith that was planted in the seedbed of expectation. This happened as I was writing this chapter in *Spiritual COVID*, so I will not use the actual names of the individuals involved. An individual who I know well was diagnosed with COVID. The person was admitted into the hospital because the physical condition continued to spiral downward. It wasn't long before that person had to be intubated. The prognosis was not good. After almost two months, the family had gathered in their loved one's hospital room to hear their doctor suggest that all life-giving assistance be removed and to let things take its course. His suggestion was turned down by the family. When the doctor left the room, the spouse of the patient called out that person's name in a loud voice. For the first time in a long time, the patient responded by head turning toward the person who had called out the name and stared in that direction. This is one of those "but God moments."

I am excited to be able to report that this individual is now home, weak but getting stronger every day. This family not only believed God can heal; they expected God to heal their loved one. Many were praying who believe God heals, but some did not expect this person would be healed because the condition was so grave, and the medical prognosis was less than encouraging. Faith planted in the seedbed of expectation transforms the ordinary into the extraordinary.

Believing for something without expecting it to happen may give us an appearance of being godly, but that is all it is, an appearance. "Having a form of godliness but denying the power. And from such people turn away" (2 Timothy 3:5 NKJV). Could it be possible that we are the kind of people that others need to stay away from? Let me say something that I have said many times already, but it needs to be said until we hear it in our innermost being. This last season we have entered is a season where we not only believe that God will do great things among us; we are expecting God to do great things.

THE IMPORTANCE OF ASSEMBLING OURSELVES TOGETHER

"And let us not neglect our meeting together, as some people do, but encourage one another, especially now that the day of his return is drawing near" (Hebrews 10:25 NLT). The human family was created for community, not isolation. The church family (believers) is no exception. Nothing, and I mean absolutely nothing, can replace our coming together as a body. The phrase "no man is an island" expresses the idea that human beings do not do well when isolated from others. People need to be part of a community to thrive (English poet John Donne, 1572–1631).

The coronavirus pandemic has certainly created all kinds of challenges for every aspect of society: That includes the church as well. As usual, the unusual brings out the innovative spirit of people. We have found all kinds of ways and methods to communicate the gospel message that deviates from that to which we are accustomed. I'm sure more ideas of how we can share the message of Christ will come to the forefront before this is over. I'm for redeeming the time and using anything at our disposal to share the Living Lord with a dying world. Christ is our only hope.

With that said, we must never forget our biblical mandate. We must never neglect the assembling of ourselves together. The church was created for community. We are designed to touch, embrace, behold one another face-to-face, pray together, laugh and cry together, to do life as a community of faith—together. This is intrinsic in our new creation's nature. No matter how beneficial technology has become, we must never allow it to replace human encounter, especially in this last season.

In trying to create a fan environment for professional athletes during the COVID pandemic, the sports world came up with a game plan. They placed cardboard cutouts of people in the stands accompanied by canned people noise. In my opinion, it does not help the optics at all. If anything, it detracts even more. I have not talked to a person yet who likes or thinks it helps or enhances the game. No matter how humanlike you can make a cardboard cutout, it will never replace the presence of an actual person.

The church has copied this concept to some degree. I don't think we have gone as far as making cardboard cutouts of people and placing them in our auditoriums, accompanied with a mechanized "amen." Then again, some churches may have. We have become a WOKE church. We have allowed man-made events to become a substitute for God-inspired moments. This is all eliminated when we not only believe God will do something miraculous; we expect him to do something out of the ordinary. This last season we have entered is a season of expectation.

Fake people in the stands of a sporting event will not add life to the event or inspire the players any more than fake people in the auditorium chairs of a church building give life to a service. God intends for his people to gather on a regular basis. We must never neglect meeting together. This pandemic that we find ourselves in has created a resurgence of small groups. We will discuss this reactivation of small group life in chapter 5.

I heard a pastor say recently that his church may never go back to having physical meetings because their virtual services are so well received by his people. Like I said earlier, I'm all in when it comes to using whatever we have at our disposal to spread the gospel but not to the exclusion of our biblical mandate of gathering, as the manner of some. Our gathering together is even more important as we see the Day of the Lord approaching (Hebrews 10:25 NKJV).

WHEN BELIEVING AND EXPECTING JOIN HANDS

Jesus and his disciples had just returned from Gadara where Jesus had delivered a man from demonic possession. Excitement was in the air as a large group of people surrounded Jesus as he walked along the narrow streets creating a natural jostling among those in the crowd. The physical touching that is taking place as they walked did not get Jesus's attention, but he is about to be touched by someone's faith. This touch would get his undivided attention: believing and expecting are about to join hands.

"Who touched my robe?" (Mark 5:30 NLT). Jesus's question got everyone's attention. There was a huge crowd surrounding them; everyone was touching him. Why would he ask, "Who touched me?" It wasn't the physical touching that got Jesus's attention. Jesus felt this woman's faith touch him, and he knew healing power had gone out of him.

The woman who was healed from the issue of blood had been fighting this battle for twelve years. The Bible says she had suffered at the hands of many doctors and had spent everything she had to pay her medical bills. She had gotten no better. In fact, she had gotten worse (Mark 5:26 NLT). Then she heard about Jesus.

We are about to see that this woman not only believed she would be healed if she touched Jesus; she expected to be healed when she touched him. She believed she would be healed, and she expected to be healed. You can have faith without expectation, but you can't have expectation without having faith. Expectation is the seedbed for miracles to happen.

"When she heard about Jesus, she came behind Him in the crowd and touched His garment" (Mark 5:27 NKJV). She heard, then she responded by touching. Romans 10:17 says: "So then faith comes by hearing" (Romans 10:17 NKJV). When this woman heard that it was Jesus who had attracted this crowd, faith began to rise inside of her. She began to talk to herself: "If only I may touch His clothes, I shall be made well" (Mark 5:28 NKJV). Her expectation of being healed has now joined hands with believing she would be healed. One more time, you can have faith without expectation, but you can't have expectation without having faith. This has been said several times already, but I am convinced it cannot be said enough.

Self-talk is something most of us know a lot about. People talk to themselves on a regular basis, whether they are aware of it or not. It is perfectly OK to talk to yourself. Sometimes it is good to talk to somebody who has good sense. Surely you know that I am being facetious: Not about talking to yourself but talking to someone who has some sense. What we say to ourselves is important, because we can talk ourselves out of the very thing we are believing for.

All her options for being healed have been taken away. There are no more doctors to see, and if there were, she has spent all her money. She was actually in a good place. When Jesus becomes our only hope, we are set up for a miracle. It has been said that when you have nothing left but you and Jesus, you have just enough to start over. This woman's life is about to be changed forever. Her hand of faith is full of expectation as she reaches out and touches the robe of Jesus. What follows is a shouting moment: "Immediately the fountain of her blood was dried up, and she felt in her body that she was healed of the affliction" (Mark 5: 29 NKJV). Immediately!

In response to this woman's touch, Jesus said, "Who touched My clothes?" (Mark 5:30 NKJV). What made this touch different from those of the crowd was the healing power that Jesus knew had gone out of him. Jesus can always be touched by our faith. This story really makes Hebrews 11:6 come alive. "But without faith it is impossible to please Him, for he who comes to God must believe that He is and that He is a rewarder of those who diligently seek Him" (Hebrews 11:6 NKJV). It pleases our heavenly Father when we come to him in faith that is filled with expectation.

The disciples reacted to what Jesus said as you would expect anyone to react in this situation. "Jesus, just in case you haven't noticed, this is a huge crowd; everyone is touching you. Why would you ask such a question?" Jesus will always recognize and respond to a faith touch. When Jesus turned around to see who had touched him, he made eye contact with the woman who had been healed. She fell at his feet and poured out her heart. She told Jesus the whole truth.

Jesus said to her, "Daughter, your faith has made you well. Go in peace. Your suffering is over" (Mark 5:34 NLT). This is a wonderful story about what can happen when believing and expecting join hands.

This last season the church has entered will be a season of expectation. Our problem and struggle has not been about believing God can and will do miracles, signs, and wonders among us; we haven't expected him to do these things. That day is over. In this last season before Christ's return, not only is the church believing God will do incredible things among us; we are expecting him to do incredible things in and through us.

A NEW NORMAL

If anything grates against my nerves more than anything else, it is the catchphrase that is being used to describe our day—"This is the new normal." I really cannot explain to you why I have such a strong disdain for this catchphrase, but I do. Maybe I don't like it because it means conforming to a standard that I don't agree with or like. If something conforms to a general pattern, standard, or average, we describe it as normal. Over time the standard can change. What is believed to be normal today can be seen as abnormal tomorrow.

Nonetheless, I will use this catchphrase to describe this last season the church has entered. The church is experiencing a new normal. This last season is a time of not only believing; it is a season of expectation. The supernatural has become natural for those who believe God can and expect that God will. A hand of faith filled with expectation will always touch the heart of God.

This last season the church has entered can be described as a season of believing and expecting. What are you believing God for? Has your expectancy joined hands with your faith? This is not something that will happen automatically or easily. It must be intentional on our part. I'm reminded of the time when Jesus came down from the mountain of transfiguration with his disciples Peter, James, and John. He saw a crowd gathered around the other disciples, and some religious teachers of the law were arguing with them. When Jesus asked them what they were arguing about, a man in the crowd spoke up. He told Jesus that his son was possessed by an evil spirit and that He had brought him to the disciples so they could cast the evil spirit out: But they could not. Then the father said to Jesus, "Have mercy on us and help us, if you can" (Mark 9:22 NLT). Jesus's response to the boy's father was straight and mater-of-fact. "What do you mean, 'If I can? Anything is possible if a person believes'" (Mark 9:23 NLT). Pay close attention to what the father says to Jesus. "I do believe, but help me overcome my unbelief" (Mark 9:24 NLT).

How is it possible to believe and have unbelief at the same time? This father believed Jesus could heal his son. This is why he had brought him to Jesus in the first place. But his expectation for his son to be healed was low. Does this sound familiar? The disciples could not heal him. His son had been this way since he was a small boy, so the father was having a hard time expecting what he was believing for. His hand of faith was empty of expectation.

For those who have the audacity to reach out and touch God with hands of faith filled with expectation, they will not be disappointed in this last season. This is a season of expectation. Expect it.

THE CHURCH IS
WAKING UP

There is so much angst and animosity regarding the church because we have not consistently lived up to what we say we believe. When I was growing up, I heard this quote on a regular basis. "What you do speaks so loudly, I can't hear what you're saying" (Ralph Waldo Emerson). Make no mistake about it; how we live reveals what we really believe. Maybe we would make great strides in impacting our homes, communities, country, and the world if we would flesh out these words: "Live what you believe so others will believe what you live" (Christine Caine). A dying world desperately needs to meet a living God. The only God some will see is the one who lives in you and me.

In the eighth chapter of Luke's Gospel, we have the story of a man named Jairus, whose twelve-year old daughter was at the point of death. This desperate father came to Jesus for help. Before they could reach Jairus's home, someone came with the news of his daughter's death. Jesus encourages Jairus to keep believing no matter what the report is. When they arrived at the home of Jairus, Jesus said: "Do not weep, she is not dead, but sleeping" (Luke 8:52 NKJV). Jesus takes the hand of the little girl, wakes her up with his voice, then tells her to get up. This is the story in capsule form.

What you are about to read is not an exposition of this text. I am using this story as an analogy to describe what I believe is happening to the church in this last season. God is taking his church by the hand and waking her up. The church has not died; she has been asleep. The church had been intubated, but she is waking up.

THE CHURCH HAS BEEN SICK

Jesus had just returned from Gadara, where he delivered a man possessed by a legion of demons. The demons begged Jesus not to send them into the abyss but to allow them to enter a herd of pigs grazing nearby. Jesus gave his consent, and the demon-possessed pigs ran violently down the steep bank into the water and drowned. You could say the pigs committed *sooie-side*. This is the first mention of *deviled ham* (Luke 8:31–33 NKJV).

A multitude of people were waiting on the banks of the Sea of Galilee to greet Jesus and his disciples on their return from Gadara. Among them was a leader in the local synagogue, a man named Jairus. His need to see Jesus was different from the rest who were in the crowd that day. His twelve-year old daughter was very sick. "[He] came and fell at Jesus' feet, pleading with him to come home with him. His only daughter, who was about twelve years old, was dying" (Luke 8:41–42 NLT). As Jesus sets out for the home of Jairus, he is stopped in his tracks by a touch of faith from a woman who is also at the end of her rope. She is desperate, and she knew her only hope was Jesus.

When I say the church has been sick for a while, I am not saying or insinuating that the church has not done anything good or has not had seasons where it has done incredible things. What I am saying is that the church has been on the decline for a while. This coronavirus pandemic has only sped up the falling away. Every report I have read, published by various denominations, reports the decline that is taking place in their denominational ranks. Fewer and fewer people are attending church services.

Most local churches are consistent at being inconsistent. Usually when new leadership is installed, the church will have a momentary spurt of life. But it does not take long for familiarity to kick in, and things decline again, waiting for the next fresh leadership change. The average stay of a pastor in a local church is 3.6 years (Lifeway Research). When I entered the ministry almost fifty years ago, the average stay of a pastor in my denomination was eighteen months. This speaks volumes about the health of most local churches. I think the word *sick* is a good word to use in describing the church before this last season we have just entered. The church will not die because it cannot die. The true church is the apple of God's eye.

As you continue reading, keep in mind that I am using this story as an analogy between Jairus's sick daughter and the church. Like Jairus's daughter, the church has been sick. But God is raising her in this last season. The church is waking up.

THE REPORT—YOUR DAUGHTER IS DEAD

Before Jesus gets to the home of Jairus, he is stopped dead in his tracks by the touch of faith. That is right—faith. We introduced this lady to you in the last chapter. Her faith filled with expectation was able to get Jesus's undivided attention. Jesus will never ignore the combination of faith and expectation. This woman had spent everything she had on physicians over the last twelve years. She and her bank account had the same problem; they both were empty. In her desperation she risked it all by reaching out and touching Jesus: the Great Physician. Immediately, the bleeding she was experiencing stopped. Jesus knew someone had touched him in faith because he felt healing power go out from him (Luke 8:46 NLT).

Put yourself in the sandals of this desperate father. You need Jesus, and you need him now! Any delay could be fatal for his twelve-year old daughter. I am sure he is a little agitated because their progress is being impeded by someone with a lesser problem.

This lady certainly needs help, but His daughter is at the point of death. I am sure Jairus was thinking, "We need to go, and we need go now!" Remember, his daughter is at the point of death. To get a vivid picture of his daughter's condition, imagine yourself on a commercial flight. As the airplane approaches the destination where you will be getting off, the stewardess says over the loudspeaker: "Please buckle your seatbelts. We will be landing in approximately fifteen minutes. Thank you for flying with us. Welcome to Dallas!" For Jairus's daughter it will be: "Welcome to—."

While Jesus was speaking to the woman who was miraculously healed when she touched him, a messenger comes with some bad news for Jairus. "Your daughter is dead. There's no use troubling the Teacher now" (Luke 8:49 NLT). I personally have heard these words spoken to me. It will rock you to your core. Nothing, and I mean absolutely nothing, can wreck you emotionally like losing a child. The delay had been costly.

When Jesus heard what had happened, he said to this grief-stricken father, "Don't be afraid. Just have faith, and she will be healed" (Luke 8:50 NLT). Jesus told Jairus to keep on believing. What Jesus said to this grieving father seems insensitive. His only daughter has just died, and Jesus tells him to keep believing.

Let's go back to the picture we are painting with this story. Many are losing or have lost hope that the church will survive. Some critics and skeptics are saying the church is as good as dead: It has lost its voice of influence and is no longer relevant in the world. There has always been a mocking spirit among unbelievers toward the community of faith, but this spirit has intensified in the last few years. Some are not only rooting for the demise of the church; they are advocating for its annihilation all together.

When I first entered the ministry, the local church was still the main social gathering place for most communities. Little by little it has been replaced with little league baseball, school activities and programs, community events, and a plethora of other happenings. These same events now compete against Sunday services; and they seem to be winning. We must be honest and ask ourselves, has the church seen its better days? Has the church gotten so sick that it will never recover? By all appearances, it seems like it has. Do not be deceived into thinking a church has closed just because you see a locked building where a church used to meet. You can close a building, but you cannot close the church. The building is not the church. We have substituted going to a church building for being the church outside the building.

These questions and questions like these are depressing to someone who loves the church. To those who feel there is no hope for the church, I will remind you of what Jesus told Jairus: "Do not be afraid, *only believe*, and she (the church) will be made well" (Luke 8:50 NKJV; emphasis added). The story is far from being over.

THE LORD IS WAKING UP HIS CHURCH

When Jesus arrived at the home of Jairus, he finds it filled with people weeping and wailing. He said to those mourning, "Stop the weeping! She isn't dead; she's only asleep" (Luke 8:52 NLT). The people went from weeping over the little girl to laughing at Jesus. The Bible says they ridiculed him for what he said. "They knew she had died" (Luke 8:53 NLT). Jesus did not permit any of these unbelievers inside the home. The only people who were allowed to come inside were Peter, John, James, and the little girl's father and mother.

"Then Jesus took her by the hand and said in a loud voice, 'My child, get up!' And at that moment her life returned, and she immediately stood up" (Luke 8:54–55 NLT)! Jesus told her parents to give her something to eat. You can imagine how amazed and awestruck Jairus and his wife must have been when their daughter opened her eyes and stood up.

If we could hear the voice of heaven speaking to the church in this last season, it may sound something like this: "Church, it is time to rise up and fulfill the assignment you have been given." The church may have been asleep for a while but do not confuse sleep with death. When we talk about the awakening of the church, the world is laughing because it is convinced the church is dead. I have some great news for you. The Lord's church is not only waking up; his church is standing up!

Dorman Duggan, a dear pastor friend of mine, has been hosting a weekly pastor's meeting for almost forty-years. This group meets every Tuesday at his church facilities from 10:00 a.m. until noon. I have had the joy of being a part of this group for the last twenty-three years. We do not follow an order of service. Our meeting is usually kicked off with these words, "What are you hearing the Lord say?" Someone will begin by sharing what they feel God is saying to them and before we know it, the two hours have flown by. Not a person in this meeting has not experienced a decline in church attendance, yet they are filled with expectation and excitement. They too believe that we have entered the last season and are convinced it will be a glorious time for the Lord's church. The Lord is waking up his bride.

GOD HAS NOT RESCINDED HIS HEAVENLY MANDATE

"And let us not neglect our meeting together, as some people do, but encouraging one another, especially now that the day of his return is drawing near" (Hebrews 10:25 NLT). I briefly mentioned in chapter 3 about hearing a pastor say that his church may never return to physically gathering again because their virtual services seem to be working so well. I believe that irreparable harm will be done to the unique fabric of the family of God if virtual gatherings become the only means of coming together.

I embrace using everything we have at our disposal to get the good news of Jesus Christ out to a world that is hopelessly lost. And what is the good news? The good news is not that Jesus lived and died. The good news is that Jesus died and now lives. Accepting and receiving Jesus Christ as one's Lord and Savior is a person's only hope. Once a person has a new birth experience, he or she needs the physical environment of the spiritual family to mature and develop in his or her faith. Without that physical connection with the family of faith, there will always be something missing in an individual's spiritual development. Like all of humanity, the family of faith was created for physical community life, not virtual. This is why we must never forsake our physical assembling.

The heart of our heavenly Father for his family is that we do not neglect our assembling together, especially as we see the day of his return approaching. Why is it important for the family of God to physically come together? Isn't virtual gathering good enough? After all, we have all this incredible technology that is available to us. Think about this. How would you feel if the only way you could spend time with the ones you love was through some mechanical feed? It might be OK for a brief time, but it would not take long before it would not satisfy the longing of your soul for a physical touch, a hug, a kiss, and the list goes on. God never intended for any of us to live the Christian life alone. Christian community is simply sharing a common life in Christ. No matter how you are wired— introvert, extrovert, socially adept or socially awkward—something in our soul longs for meaningful relationships with other humans. God created us for community.

When the COVID pandemic first became an issue, like many churches, we moved our services to the back parking lot of our church facilities. Because we live in the Panhandle of Texas, wind can be an issue. During our first service outside, my plexiglass pulpit was blown over by the wind, and it shattered into pieces. That was not on the same level as the parting of the Red Sea, but I took it as a sign for us to move back inside the building.

Holding services outside was kind of exciting for our people at first. It was something new. Folks could sit in their vehicles, sip their coffee or morning juice, and munch on their breakfast food snacks while they were still snuggled in their pajamas. It was difficult for those of us who were leading the service to tell if the people in their vehicles were singing, or how involved they were in the service. Ministry time was very impersonal as well. We did see some of our neighbors come outside of their homes when they heard the singing and preaching. They participated in the service from their front porches. You could tell they were hungry for fellowship and human contact too.

While I was preaching, the people would honk their horns to express their approval, or they would flash their headlights. This was their way of saying, amen. Some may have honked their horns simply because they could. I know my people. When the service ended, the people would drive to the west side of the facilities and place their gifts in the mailbox that is located underneath a drive-through. After our second week of having our services outside in the back parking lot, our people had their fill. Even though we were in proximity to one another in our vehicles, we were still not together. It was time to go back inside where we could "be together."

If there has been anything that we have learned from this COVID pandemic season, it is the importance of physically coming together as the family of God. The church in this last season is waking up to the truth of how important it is for believers to be with one another on a regular basis—even more so as we see the day of the Lord approaching.

KEEP BELIEVING WHAT GOD SAYS EVEN IF YOU CANNOT SEE WHAT GOD IS DOING

When Jesus arrived at the home of Jairus, a crowd had gathered to mourn and weep over the loss of this little girl. Jesus basically says to them what he said to Jairus when he received the news that his daughter had died. "Stop the weeping! She isn't dead; she's only asleep. But the crowd laughed at him because *they all knew she had died*" (Luke 8:52–53 NLT; emphasis added). Sometimes what we are believing God for is not supported by what we see. There are times when we have no sight to support our faith.

All the mourners laughed at Jesus for saying what he did because they were convinced Jairus's daughter had died. After all, they could see that she was no longer breathing. What Jesus said could not be supported by what the people could see. They said she has died, but Jesus said she is asleep.

"Then Jesus took her by the hand and said in a loud voice, 'My child, get up!' And at that moment her life returned, and she immediately stood up! Then Jesus told them to give her something to eat. Her parents were overwhelmed by this miracle moment, but Jesus insisted that they not tell anyone what had happened" (Luke 8:54–56 NLT). Can you imagine what the people outside were saying to one another when they heard Jesus say in a loud voice, "My child, get up." Jesus said to give her something to eat. Dead people don't eat. I would love to have seen their faces when they saw Mr. and Mrs. Jairus's little girl running around, playing like twelve-year-old children do. Jairus and his wife were overcome with joy to see their daughter filled with new life. I am sure the mumbling and mocking that had been going on in the crowd had come to a screeching halt. The quietness must have been deafening as the people shook their heads in shock and unbelief.

Jesus told the little girl's parents not to tell anyone what had happened. This seems kind of weird. It is on the same level as "keep on believing" when there is no reason to believe. How are they going to hide what had just happened? Many people had witnessed the death and resurrection of their daughter. I am sure this neighborhood was buzzing with the news about Jairus's daughter being raised from the dead by Jesus. How in the world can you keep something like this quiet?

Because the crowd of mourners did not believe, they were not allowed to see what Peter, John, James, Jairus, and his wife witnessed. Those who dare to believe in this last season, no matter how hopeless things may appear, will be able to see and experience what others are not allowed to see.

I am convinced that this story is a beautiful picture of this last season we have entered. Things that appear as if they have died will live again. Like Jairus's daughter, Jesus is bringing new life to the church. The church is waking up—even amid all the mocking and ridicule by unbelievers.

THE DARKER THE NIGHT, THE BRIGHTER THE LIGHT

When I look around and see the moral bankruptcy of this great nation that I love so dearly, and the deteriorating social condition of our country, the words of Isaiah become as fresh to me as if he had written them today. "Woe to those who call evil good, and good evil; Who put darkness for light, and light for darkness; Who put bitter for sweet, and sweet for bitter!" (Isaiah 5:20 NKJV). We are doing the very thing we were warned not to do. In many sectors of life, bad is being called good, and good is considered bad. If you had told me five years ago that we would be where we are today in America, I would not have believed you. Things seem to be spiraling further and further out of control. One cannot help but wonder if humanity has passed fail-safe—a place of no return.

When I was growing up, it was not uncommon to hear someone say during tough times, "Cheer up, things could get worse." One guy responded by saying, "I cheered up, and sure enough, things got worse." During this dark season that we are in right now, my counsel to you is, cheer up, it could get darker. As a matter of fact, I have an unction the darkness is going to get darker. Do not panic if it does, because the true church is going to get brighter. The church is rising in her new creation identity, and her light will dispel the darkness. Darkness is no competition for light.

The words that Jesus spoke to Jairus are the words the church desperately needs to hear today—"Keep believing." This is not easy to do when you have no sight to support your faith. But always keep this in mind, Jesus would not tell us to do something if we could not do it. The Lord never told us it would be easy to trust him. We need to keep trusting him no matter how dark things may appear.

God dispelled darkness in the beginning of time with the spoken word: "Then God said, 'Let there be light,' and there was light. And God saw that the light was good. Then he separated the light from the darkness. God called the light "day" and the darkness "night" (Genesis 1:3–5 NLT). I love these words: "The evening passed and morning came" (Genesis 1:6 NLT).

The greatest enemy of darkness is light. "[You] are the light of the world. A city that is set on a hill cannot be hidden. Let your light so shine before men, that they may see your good works and glorify your Father in heaven" (Matthew 5:14–16 NKJV; emphasis added). When you rise in your new creation identity, you become your enemy's greatest foe. Light is the intimidator, not darkness. Do not run from the darkness in this last season. Run to it. The darker it is, the brighter you shine.

"For we are not fighting against flesh-and-blood enemies, but against evil rulers and authorities of the unseen world, *against mighty powers in this dark world*, and against evil spirits in the heavenly places" (Ephesians 6:12 NLT; emphasis added). Satan wants you to think that your light (life) is too dim to make a difference. He wants you to believe that he is unconquerable when all the while he is terrified of your light. Light is his kryptonite. When we let our light shine, it exposes him for what he is, who he is, and his weaknesses and tactics. If there has ever been a time in the history of the world when light is needed, it is in this last season. No matter how dim light may be, it will always displace darkness. Always! Maybe this is what Ann Frank had in mind when she said, "Look at how a single candle can both defy and define the darkness."

When God began speaking creation into existence, there was darkness before light. "And that is what happened. God made this space to separate the waters of the earth from the waters of the heavens. God called the space 'sky.' And evening (darkness) passed and morning (light) came, marking the second day" (Genesis 1:7 NLT; emphasis added). This is very significant. In the very beginning of time, God established an irrevocable principal; light will always displace darkness. If darkness had been created first, it would have the ability to extinguish light.

In Paul's first letter to the church in Thessalonica, he reminded them of their identities as born-from-above believers. His words to them are appropriate for us in this last season, as we see the day of the Lord's return approaching. "But *you aren't in the dark* about these things, dear brothers and sisters, and you won't be surprised when the day of the Lord comes like a thief. For *you are all children of the light and of the day*; we don't belong to darkness and night. So be on your guard, not asleep like the others. Stay alert and be clearheaded. Night is the time when people sleep and drinkers get drunk. But *let us who live in the light* be clearheaded, protected by the armor of faith and love, and wearing as our helmet the confidence of our salvation" (1 Thessalonians 5:4–8 NLT; emphasis added). We really need to allow these words to penetrate deep within us as we navigate our way through this dark season. As children of the light and of the day, we are shielded by the armor of faith and love. This is important to know because the world is bent on silencing the church—even eradicating it if it possibly can.

Why does the world have so much visceral hatred for the church? Because we are light, and our light exposes the nefarious acts and deeds that are being perpetrated in the dark. Jesus talked about this last season and what we can expect. He said, "Sin will be rampant everywhere, and the love of many will grow cold" (Matthew 24:12 NLT). In this last season we have discovered how iniquitous many of our elected leaders have become. If there has ever been a time in history where the church needs to let its light shine, it is now!

THE LORD'S PRAYER FOR US

One day the disciples asked Jesus to teach them how to pray as John had taught his disciples (Luke 11:1 NKJV). Jesus gave them this prayer template. "When you pray, here is what you say:" (Luke 11:2 NKJV). What follows is what most people call the Lord's prayer. In reality, it is not the Lord's prayer because Jesus could not pray this prayer; for it says, "Forgive us our sins, as we forgive those who sin against us" (Luke 11:4 NLT). Since Jesus is sinless, he cannot pray this prayer. This is actually the model prayer, and it can be found in Matthew chapter 6 and in Luke chapter 11. The Lord's prayer is found in John chapter 17.

We were included in the Lord's prayer long before we were ever born. "I do not pray for these alone [speaking of his disciples], but also for those who will believe in Me through their word" (John 17:20 NKJV; emphasis added). Think about this, Jesus prayed for you before you were ever in your mother's womb. How awesome is that?

Listen to what Jesus prayed: "I have given them your word. And the world hates them because they do not belong to the world, just as I do not belong to the world. I'm not asking you to take them out of the world, but to keep them safe from the evil one. They do not belong to this world any more than I do. Make them holy by your truth; teach them your word, which is truth. *Just as you sent me into the world, I am sending them into the world*" (John 17:13–18 NLT; emphasis added).

Pay close attention to what Jesus said about how the world sees and feels about believers. The world hates true believers because they are not a part of the world's system. We are *in the world*, but *we are not of the world*. Jesus did not ask the Father to remove us from this world. He prayed for the Father to keep us safe and to protect us from the evil one. Then he reveals the reason we are to remain in this world for this season: "I am sending them into the world for the same reason you sent me into the world" (John 17:18 NLT). We are to bring the light of life to a dark and dying world—a world that is hopelessly lost without Christ.

Our purpose for remaining in this world during this last season is to invade the darkness and bring hope to the souls of humanity. The world hates us the same way it hates Jesus. Light exposes what is being done in the dark, and darkness does not like exposure. No matter how dark things may appear or become, we must never forget what the word of God says: "Darkness can never extinguish light" (John 1:5 NLT).

"The Word [Jesus] gave life to everything that was created, and *his life brought light to everyone*. The light shines in darkness, and the darkness can never extinguish it" (John 1:4–5 NLT; emphasis added). Light will always dispel darkness no matter how dark it may be or how dim the light. I find it interesting that the definition of darkness, "is the partial or total absence of light" (Merriam Webster). If darkness is the absence of light, then the presence of light sends darkness into hiding. If you walk into a dark room and flip the light switch on, where does the darkness go? I do not know either, but I do know how to get the dark to return. Turn the light switch off.

Jesus said, "I am the light of the world. If you follow me, you won't have to walk in darkness, because you will have the light that leads to life" (John 8:12 NLT). This is how we navigate in this dark world that we find ourselves in; we follow Jesus's lead.

THE DAY OF THE LORD'S RETURN IS DRAWING NEAR

The church is waking up in this last season with a fresh anointing and a burning desire to make Christ known to a hostile and sin-sick world. If there has ever been a time in the history of humankind when good news needs to be shared and heard, it is now. Let me remind us all once again what the good news is. The good news is not that Jesus lived and died. The good news is that Jesus died and now lives. Not only is he alive; he is coming back to receive those who have prepared themselves for his return. The day of his return is drawing near.

The words Paul wrote to Timothy describing the season of the Lord's return sound as if they were written today. Read the following passage of scripture slowly and see if it fits our day and time we are living in. "You should know this Timothy, that in the last days there will be very difficult times. For people will love only themselves and their money. They will be boastful and proud, scoffing at God, disobedient to their parents, and ungrateful. They will consider nothing sacred. They will be unloving and unforgiving; they will slander others and have no self-control. They will be cruel and hate what is good. They will betray their friends, be reckless, be puffed up with pride, and love pleasure rather than God. They will act religious, but they will reject the power that could make them godly. Stay away from people like that!" (2 Timothy 3:1–5 NLT).

Here is what Peter said about the day of the Lord's coming. "Most importantly, I want to remind you that in the last days *scoffers* will come, mocking the truth and following their own desires" (2 Peter 3:3 NLT; emphasis added). I know that scoffers have been around for a long time. As a matter of fact, we can go all the way back to the Garden of Eden to find the first scoffer—Satan. His first words to Eve were, "Did God really say—" (Genesis 3:1 NLT). This is his attempt to cast doubt on the word of God. Satan was mocking what God had said to them about eating from the forbidden tree— the tree of the knowledge of good and evil.

Can you imagine the mocking and ridicule Noah must have experienced when he was building the ark? He was surrounded by people who were laughing and mocking him for simply following God's instructions. You can hear their scoffing: "Rain? It has never rained! You have lost your mind, Noah." Things did change when it started raining. "For forty days the floodwaters grew deeper, covering the ground and lifting the boat high above the earth. As the waters rose higher and higher above the ground, the boat floated safely on the surface. Finally, the water covered even the highest mountains on the earth, rising more than twenty-two feet above the highest peaks. *All the living things on earth died*—birds, domestic animals, wild animals, small animals that scurry along the ground, *and all the people*. Everything that breathed and lived on dry land died" (Genesis 7:17–22 NLT; emphasis added). The only ones who survived were the ones who had obeyed God's word—Noah and those with him in the boat.

Scoffers have always been a part of this fallen world. But in this last season the scoffing will increase, just like Peter said it would. Because thousands of years have passed since Christ ascended into heaven, there will be an increase in scoffing by unbelievers as the day of the Lord approaches. They will make fun of and question the coming of the Lord. Anyone who believes that Christ's return is imminent will be ridiculed and labeled as being mentally unstable. "Where is the promise of His coming? For since the fathers fell asleep, all things continue as they were from the beginning of creation" (2 Peter 3:4 NKJV) Things will change when it starts to rain.

Just in case you have not noticed, it is beginning to rain. The noise from all the chaos that is taking place in the world today is waking up the sleeping church. "The Christian world is in a deep sleep. Nothing but a loud voice can waken them out of it" (George Whitefield, 1739). These words were spoken over 280 years ago. They are now being fulfilled. The church has heard the loud voice of the Spirit of God and is rising in her new creation identity, to prepare the way for the imminent return of the Lord.

"Take no part in the worthless deeds of evil and darkness; instead expose them. It is shameful even to talk about the things that ungodly people do in secret. *But their evil intentions will be exposed when the light shines on them, for the light makes everything visible.* This is why it is said, 'Awake, O sleeper, rise up from the dead, and *Christ will give you light*'" (Ephesians 5:11–14 NLT; emphasis added). The Lord's church is not only waking up; the church is rising and becoming what she was designed to be from the very beginning— the light of hope for a dark and lost world. As the heavenly Father sent his Son into this world to be the light for all of humanity, he is sending us into the darkness to be light, so lost souls can find their way to God.

THE CHURCH IS WOKE

I guess we could say in its truest sense, the church is woke. The church has been aroused from its sleep. The church just woke up. I am convinced that we are living in the most exciting time in the history of the world. Many of the prophets of old saw what we have today, but they could not have it. We have it, but we cannot see it. That is changing. The church is beginning to see who they are, what they have, and what they have been commissioned to do—just in time for this last season before the Lord splits the eastern skies.

Paul ends his first letter to the Thessalonians with these words: "For God chose to save us through our Lord Jesus Christ, not to pour out his anger on us. Christ died for us so that, whether we are dead or alive when he returns, we can live with him forever. *So encourage each other and build each other up, just as you are already doing*" (1 Thessalonians 5:9–11 NLT; emphasis added).

The church is waking up.

RESURGENCE OF THE SMALL HOME CHURCH

I f we have learned anything from this COVID pandemic, it is our hunger and need for human contact. God created us for community. We can now see the adverse effect isolation has had on our children by not being able to attend school. Thousands of small businesses have had to lock their doors. The majority of these will never recover. Restaurants have been decimated because they cannot open to serve their customers—inside or outside. And in many places, churches have been forbidden to meet in community.

The enemy has used this COVID pandemic as one huge distraction. Distractions can be extremely dangerous because your attention is taken away from what you need to be doing. If we get too focused on what this pandemic has taken away from us, we will not be able to see what God is raising in front of us. Sometimes it takes a loss to see what we really have. The following statement means more to me today than it did when I first heard it many years ago: When the only thing you have left is Jesus, you have just enough to start over. Jesus is always more than enough.

Jesus and his disciples were on their way to Jerusalem when they stopped at a certain village where two sisters, Mary and Martha, lived.

Martha welcomed them into her home. While Martha was busy preparing a big dinner for their guests, sister Mary was sitting at the feet of Jesus feasting on every word that came out of his mouth. Martha's busyness and Mary's idleness became the elixir for an uncomfortable moment for these two sisters. "But Martha was *distracted* by the big dinner she was preparing. She came to Jesus and said, 'Lord, doesn't it seem unfair to you that my sister just sits here while I do all the work? Tell her to come and help me'" (Luke 10:40 NLT; emphasis added). What Jesus said to Martha gives us invaluable insight into priorities. "My dear Martha, you are worried and upset over all these details! *There is only one thing worth being concerned about.* Mary has discovered it, and it will not be taken away from her" (Luke 10:41–42 NLT; emphasis added). Mary was attracted by worship, and Martha was distracted by work. When it comes to our priorities, nothing, absolutely nothing, should ever compete with our worship time. As important as work is, it should never take precedence over worship.

Martha was distracted by her work. To be distracted means to have one's thoughts and attention drawn away. When we are distracted, we find it very difficult to concentrate on what we need to be paying attention to. A great professional golfer once said, "You can always find a distraction if you're looking for one" (Tom Kite).

This COVID pandemic season has been one big distraction. By saying this I am not making light of or diminishing the horrible consequences this disease storm has caused. It has been very costly in lives as well as to people's livelihoods. The enemy has used it to distract and draw us away from what we need to be paying attention to—what God is doing in and through his glorious church.

Let me give you an example. For months we were told that we must hunker down, (self- quarantine), and not gather with anyone outside of our homes. Then we were told it was OK to assemble with others if it was kept to a specific number. During this time of isolation, the church became aware of the importance of our heavenly mandate found in the book of Hebrews. "And let us not neglect our meeting together, as some people do, but encourage one another, especially now that the day of his return is drawing near" (Hebrews 10:25 NLT). It is impossible for government to legislate the word of God out of our lives. No matter what happens in this world, the word of God will never be repealed. There is no room for discussion or debate about this. Case closed!

With the passing of time Christians began to miss the personal interaction they need with one another, so they started assembling in small groups. Because of the distraction the pandemic created, we were unable to see at first what was happening. The Acts 2 pattern of church began to reappear right before our very eyes, and most of us did not even see it. It is a resurgence of the small home church.

THE ACTS 2 HOME CHURCH PATTERN

In case someone may be thinking that I am saying, or implying, that the small home church will replace the large church paradigm that most of us have known for so long, I will say it one more time: The large church paradigm will more than likely continue in some shape and form, even though many leaders of some large churches have gone on record saying they are considering ways they can do church differently. There has been too much financial investment for these ministries, (especially the very large ones), to abandon what they have been doing. The monetary loss would be staggering. But in my opinion, the larger churches will not be as effective or as powerful in many ways as the small home church model will be in this end-time season.

I do not want to give the impression that the small home church will replace the large church. What I am saying is that this pandemic has revealed the special place the small home church will have in this last season before the return of Christ. I am convinced that people will be searching for these small home church groups with which to connect. When push comes to shove, and if persecution increases, the small in-home gathering of believers may be the way the church survives.

In this last season, there will be a return to the church being the body of Christ, (*ekklesia*: called out ones, assembly), not a particular building or facility where the church gathers. If you pay close attention as you read through the New Testament, you will notice more is said about the church as people than it does about the church as a place. "Please give my greetings to our brothers and sisters at Laodicea, and to Nympha and *the church that meets in her house*" (Colossians 4:15 NLT; emphasis added). "This letter is from Paul, a prisoner for preaching the Good News about Christ Jesus, and from our brother Timothy. I am writing to Philemon, our beloved co-worker, and to our sister Apphia, and to our fellow soldier Archippus, and to *the church that meets in your house*" (Philemon 1–2 NLT; emphasis added).

For the first three-hundred years of its existence, the church of the Lord Jesus Christ met almost exclusively in people's homes (Acts 20:20; Romans 16:5; 1 Corinthians 16:19; Colossians 4:15 NKJV). Today the church meets primarily in buildings specifically designed for religious services. Here is the point I want to make: church buildings do have some advantages, but they are not essential for numerical growth or spiritual depth. The early church possessed both these qualities, and the church's greatest period of vitality and growth until recent times was during the first two centuries. History shows the church grew the fastest when it did not have the luxury of having a central building to meet in. Do not let this historical fact slip past you. The church had its greatest growth when it did not have the help or hindrance of church buildings? Absolutely nothing is wrong with a church having a central building to meet in. We just need to keep in mind that whatever structure we choose, it exists for a purpose; structures are not an end in themselves.

Since the early church primarily met in private homes, the typical congregation was smaller rather than larger. Smaller groups can foster intimacy and accountability far better than larger group gatherings. If there is anything obvious by its absence in our churches today, it is intimacy and accountability. Many churches have gotten so big that the people do not know each other. Here is a sadder note. In most churches we do not want to know people or want people to know us. The motivation behind many people becoming a part of a large church is that they can hide. They want the benefits they feel the large church has to offer, but they do not want any responsibility or accountability. We have filled our buildings with spectators, when we need participators.

ADVANTAGES OF SMALL HOME CHURCHES

Meeting in private homes is not commanded nor is it forbidden. It is acceptable if people do or if they do not. It is a personal choice. Small home churches do have advantages that large churches do not have. Smaller groups can steward their resources better; discovering and maturing in one's new creation identity will be much easier—expansion is not time consuming and expensive, and intimacy and accountability are easier to foster.

STEWARDING RESOURCES

Using private homes as the early church did is a much better way to steward resources. One of the great advantages of not having a large mortgage debt, upkeep and maintenance budget, and burdensome overhead expenses is that we do not have to consult our budget to see if we can do what God tells us to do. Smaller groups meeting in private homes can steward resources much better than a larger church can.

Can you imagine how much money is being spent by churches every year on buildings, and on the upkeep and maintenance of these buildings? The amount must be staggering! Is this the best way to steward our resources? Once again, I am not saying that having buildings for the people of faith to meet in is wrong and should be abandoned. I am purposefully raising questions to stimulate thought and to make you aware of what I see is happening in this last season before the Lord's return.

The best ways to use our financial resources are for missions, benevolence within our small groups and community, and elder support, rather than building expenses. It will certainly simplify things and give us the freedom to do whatever God tells us to do without having to consult our budgets to see if we can obey God. Maybe Confucius was not confused when he said, "Life is really simple, but we insist on making it complicated" (Confucius).

MATURING IN FAITH COMES EASIER AND QUICKER

The church family gathering in smaller groups encourages and stimulates participation, interaction, discussion, and personal ministry. Having smaller groups creates a warmer and more intimate environment for people to feel comfortable. It is more of a family atmosphere, and that is what the church is—a family. People seem to relax faster and open up easier in an intimate group setting.

Have you ever wondered how believers discovered their spiritual gift in the early days of the church? They certainly did not have a spiritual gift test they could take or a spiritual gift inventory to read and study. It was through observation by the believers in the group. This is not possible when you have hundreds or thousands of people gathering.

The interaction between members and personal involvement within the group is more natural and much easier in small, intimate group settings. A person will usually engage faster when the atmosphere is more like family. This is a great advantage that the small home church has over the traditional large church service we have become accustomed to today.

Something is engaging about being able to look one another in the eye, to see and feel one another's emotions, and to touch people. Spontaneous ministry is more likely to take place in a private home church meeting. We have put this to the test and have seen individuals open up who have not said a word in the years they have been attending big church. Most of the time they are not even aware they are participating. Engagement comes easily and naturally in a family setting.

EXPANSION AND GROWTH

When a church begins to reach more people and its membership outgrows its current facilities, it's time to move, buy, or build bigger facilities. This involves time and resources—a lot of resources. It can take several years to plan and construct facilities large enough to handle the number of people attending. Oftentimes a church will incur a lot of debt to secure adequate space for their growing congregation. This not only increases the church's debt; it increases the upkeep and maintenance budget. That puts us back into what we have worked so hard to get out of: before we can say yes to what God tells us to do, we must consult our budget to see if we can afford to do it. The dog continues to chase its tail.

When a small home church reaches an average attendance of ten to twenty people, it is time to create another small group. This takes very little time and even fewer resources. You find another private home to meet in. This can be done overnight. Since you are always developing leadership, an individual is ready to shepherd the group. A small home church has the advantage over the traditional church when it comes to expansion and growth.

You can always bring your small home church groups together on special occasions for a celebration service, to cast vision, for a mission assignment, to share testimonies of small-group life, or for a thousand other reasons to promote what God is doing. You can do this by renting a local civic center, a gymnasium, or by borrowing or renting a local church's facility to host this meeting. Bringing all your groups together on special occasions helps keep the small home church vision alive and vibrant. Small home churches have an incredible advantage over large church groups when it comes to expansion. It is also incredibly less expensive.

INTIMACY AND ACCOUNTABILITY

Even though the church is a family, it is very difficult to get to know your church family if it is large. There cannot be much intimacy if you do not know your church family. Intimacy simply means—"into-me-you-see." The format of how we conduct our large church services does not lend itself to creating an atmosphere for intimacy to be experienced or for accountability.

A natural environment for intimacy is created when a small group meets in a private home. It also becomes a natural setting for accountability to take place. Sheer numbers are the contributing factor. In smaller groups, it is easier to go deeper in Bible study and at the same time develop relationships—while socializing and having a good time.

The church is a community; therefore, the smaller gathering can become a tighter community of friends, and it will be noticed if you are not around, participating, or if you are going through a tough time. Personal ministry is more likely to happen in smaller groups.

Because one of the purposes of having smaller groups is to develop leaders for expansion, an individual's leadership skills can be developed much faster in a small home church setting than in a large church gathering.

Large church services are designed for teaching and training with the entire group in mind. This is why you never see anyone raise their hand to ask a question. Whereas small groups have a natural environment where a person can raise his or her hand or ask a hard question. Smaller groups are more focused on the individual, making it more conducive to grow in one's spiritual life.

I believe a lot of people would like to attend church but feel intimidated to visit a large church. Smaller groups present a less-threatening environment, allowing a person the opportunity to connect with people, which is the cry of the human heart—to be a part of community.

DISADVANTAGES OF SMALL HOME CHURCHES

The small home church model does have inherent dangers that must not be overlooked. It would be naive to think that all church issues will be resolved if we go to a small home church model. Do not drink the Kool-Aid. There will always be issues that must be dealt with because ministry involves people. I heard an old-timer say one time (in jest——I think), "Ministry would be great if you did not have to deal with people." Since the focus of ministry is people, there will always be challenges.

SMALL GROUPS CAN BECOME INGROWN

Since small groups are more intimate than large groups, we get comfortable with those in our small group family. It is a part of the DNA of small group life. When that happens, there can be resistance when creating more small groups becomes a reality. We do not want to break up our family, and sometimes we are reluctant to allow "new people" to join our family. We are not comfortable with outsiders. Our attention and interest can turn inward rather than outward. If that happens the group becomes ingrown, stagnant, and will eventually implode.

SMALL GROUPS CAN FAIL TO DEVELOP LEADERSHIP

Developing leadership must always be at the top of our list of priorities. People with strong leadership skills will manifest immediately. Their ability and willingness to lead will be obvious early on, while it may take a while for others. Just because someone may not manifest leadership skills immediately does not mean they will not or cannot be strong, effective leaders of small groups.

Why look for and develop leaders when there is so much interaction within the group? This is the danger that leads to failure in developing leadership. Everyone leads in their own right. When someone is leading effectively it may not be noticeable. When a sporting event is being officiated well, the referees will go unnoticed. The focus of the fans will be on the teams playing the game, not on the ones refereeing the game.

SMALL GROUPS CAN LOSE SIGHT OF SUPPORTING MISSIONS

The natural focus of attention of a small group is on the individuals in the group. This is one of the unique benefits of small group life, but it can also be the Achilles' heel for the small group. The group can lose sight of the importance of the broader picture, like supporting missions. Keeping the importance of mission support in the forefront helps prevent the group from developing tunnel vision. By keeping mission support in our conversation, the synergy between small group life and mission involvement is not lost.

SMALL GROUP LEADERSHIP CAN BECOME ROGUE

There will always be the possibility of a rogue leader steering the small group away from its intended purpose. Because this has happened on numerous occasions, primarily church-initiated small life groups, many pastors have euthanized small groups completely. This is less common in home-church start-ups. Keep in mind that anything that can happen in large church meetings can happen in small church meetings. We are dealing with people, and people are people whether they are meeting in a large group or a small group.

If we will not allow dissension and distraction that takes place in large gatherings to deter us from having church, we should not allow the same distractions to stop us from having small groups. Fear is a foe of faith, and we should never allow it to keep us from doing what God wants us to do. God has not given us *a spirit* of fear (2 Timothy 1:7 NKJV; emphasis added). Fear is a spirit, and its assignment is to rob us of the power, the love, and the peace that we have in Christ as new creation beings.

CHALLENGE OF INCORPORATING GENERATIONAL MINISTRY INTO HOME CHURCH DNA

Incorporating all ages in the life of a small group can be a challenge. Just because it is a challenge does not mean it is impossible to accomplish. A challenge to a heart filled with faith is just that—a challenge. Do not let this challenge keep you from experiencing what God has for you.

How do you incorporate the younger generation, whose cellphone charger is their umbilical cord, into the life of a small home group? Not only does the younger generation need to be heard; they need to feel emotionally, physically, and digitally safe. Welcome their doubts, anxieties, frustrations, and even their anger with God and the church. We have plenty of biblical examples of doubt and unbelief.

Small group life gives the younger generation the opportunity to engage in dialogue rather than with monologue of "churchy" anecdotes. Give them the opportunity to choose and participate in mission efforts. Keep them involved in conversation as much as possible after the group has ended its time. Do your best and let God do the rest.

There are a lot of cons to conducting healthy private home church groups, but the pros far outweigh the cons. Do not allow someone's horror story about home groups become your nightmare.

OPPOSITION TO SMALL HOME CHURCH GROUPS

I read an article the other day by an individual who is advocating the cancelation of all small private home groups. The following is the basic reason given by the author of this article why church leadership is reluctant to have or is totally against having small groups. Small groups have an unclear purpose, they are poorly led, and the teaching is not healthy, little to no scripture is taught or shared, the members are unfriendly, the group is not prepared for new arrivals, and the meeting usually ends as a gossip session.

If I understand what the author of this article is saying, the small groups they are referring to are primarily church initiated small life groups, not home-church start-ups. A large percentage of pastors are afraid small groups will become a church within the church, and collaboration between the small groups and the large group will be lost; its members become apathetic to the larger church and its mission. The resurgence I am talking about are home-church starts that remain in private homes even as they grow and expand.

IS THIS RESURGENCE OF SMALL HOME CHURCHES A SEASON OF PREPARATION FOR THE LORD'S RETURN?

I do not want to give the impression that I believe everyone needs to adopt the small private home church model. This is not going to happen—and it probably should not happen. I do want to go on record: a resurgence of small home church starts is taking place all over the world in this last season—especially in countries where religious persecution is the norm. The Christian faith is growing the fastest in countries where persecution is the greatest. Christians in these countries cannot meet in large central buildings to worship. They would be arrested, imprisoned, or killed. Their only alternative is to meet in small groups in private homes. Someday the only alternative we may have is to meet in small groups in someone's home. Do not slough this off too quickly. We could be much closer to this being a reality than we realize.

When I use the term *small home churches*, I am not talking about Life Groups that many larger churches have created for their church family to attend. Life Groups are an extension of the large church's ministry and are usually created according to age, gender, or interests. These groups are invaluable to the bonding and camaraderie that is desperately needed within the family of faith.

Small home churches on the other hand, are not extensions of a larger local church family; they are the church family that happens to meet in private homes. When a group reaches a certain number in attendance, a new group will be formed, and it too will meet in a private home. This is where the name is derived from—home church.

Is the Spirit of God using this coronavirus (COVID-19) pandemic to prepare his people for something that is coming? I am not saying he is, but I will not ignore it either. This is certainly something that must be given thought. If you had told me a few short years ago that we would be where we are today in our country, I would probably have laughed and labeled you as a conspiracy theorist. If this pandemic season has done anything, it has reminded us of something we all know —things can change on a dime.

OUTSIDE OF OUR WESTERN THINK BOX

It amazes me how many Christians do not believe that Christians meeting in a private home can legitimately be called a church. The reason this is true is because we have flipped the script. Instead of seeing people as the church, most Christians see a place as being the church.

The first church began in a home on the Day of Pentecost (Acts 2 NKJV). Gathering in someone's home became the natural place for believers to assemble for several reasons. Very few large facilities were available where the church could meet. But more importantly, persecution drove the church to meet in private homes. Those who professed faith in Christ were always at risk of being punished.

The term *church* in the New Testament was used in reference to the gathering of believers rather than the building in which they met. A church gathering can meet in a home, an outdoor location, a large building, a school, a gymnasium, or any structure suitable to corporate gatherings designed to worship God. The home church certainly can be biblical.

The first church I pastored began under a brush arbor: a few poles planted in the ground with a brush roof draped over the top. Because a place is not the church, my first church could have kept meeting under that brush arbor. It might have gotten uncomfortable after a while, but the place did not determine if it was a church or not; it was the people.

The home church is certainly not traditional, and it may not "feel" like church to those accustomed to meeting in church buildings. But this is a cultural issue, not a biblical concept. Some feel they can worship better in a large facility, while others prefer a home environment to worship in. It is about the God we worship, not the building that holds or gatherings.

Many home churches have sprouted from the seedbed of opposition to what is seen as the institutional church. This is never a legitimate reason to begin a new work. A healthy beginning is what determines the ending. This is when the time principle kicks in. Time will either vindicate you, or time will indict you: Just give it time.

One of the main concerns some have about home churches is accountability. Home churches can lack in accountability as can a larger church that is connected to a network or denomination of churches. But that can be remedied easy enough through connection with a covering body of eldership and networking with other home churches.

BIBLICAL RECORD OF HOME CHURCHES

"And when they had entered, *they went up into the upper room where they were staying*: Peter, James, John, and Andrew; Philip and Thomas; Bartholomew and Matthew; James the son of Alphaeus and Simon the Zealot; and Judas the son of James" (Acts 1:13 NKJV; emphasis added).

"And suddenly there came a sound from heaven, as of a rushing mighty wind, and *it filled the whole house* where they were sitting" (Acts 2:2 NKJV; emphasis added).

"To the beloved Apphia, Archippus our fellow soldier, and to *the church in your house*" (Philemon 1:2 NKJV; emphasis added).

"I kept back nothing that was helpful, but proclaimed it to you, and taught you publicly and from *house to house*" (Acts 20:20 NKJV; emphasis added).

"And daily in the temple, and *in every house*, they did not cease teaching and preaching Jesus as the Christ" (Acts 5:42 NKJV; emphasis added).

"The churches of Asia greet you. Aquila and Priscilla greet you heartily in the Lord, with *the church that is in their house*" (1 Corinthians 16:19 NKJV; emphasis added).

"Likewise *greet the church that is in their house*. Greet my beloved Epaenetus, who is the first fruits of Achaia to Christ" (Romans 16:5 NKJV; emphasis added).

"Greet the brethren who are in Laodicea, and Nymphas and *the church that is in his house*" (Colossians 4:15 NKJV; emphasis added).

"For where two or three are gathered together in My name, I am there in the midst of them" (Matthew 18:20 NKJV).

Ultimately, the location is less important than the functions of the church, which are to worship God, to serve him with a whole heart, to win souls, and to make disciples. There is a resurgence of the small home church in this last season.

LESSONS FROM UGANDA

H as the modern church era domesticated us as believers to the point where we have lost our wildness for the things of the Spirit? We believe supernatural things happened back in the day, but we are not convinced they happen in our day. We believe miracles can happen, but we do not expect them to happen. We have become spiritually domesticated. Modern-day religion has made us more sophisticated, educated, and inoculated, and I am afraid we have become spiritually constipated. Our entire spiritual system is stopped up.

I shared with you in the beginning of this book one of the sayings this weird coronavirus season has produced that grates on my nerves—we have a new normal. I am going to use this phrase that I abhor to describe the church in this last season. The Lord's church is experiencing a new normal. What we believe happened a long time ago but do not expect it to happen today is happening. The church is experiencing a new normal that will appear to many who are subnormal as being abnormal. Miracles, signs, and wonders are bursting out everywhere.

Several years ago, I was asked to preach the memorial service of a man I knew and respected. Before the service began, his wife handed me a note and asked if I would read it during the service. It is not uncommon for this to happen. At times I did not want to read what was given to me because I felt what I was being asked to read was not appropriate for the moment. But I have always acquiesced to the family's request. This time was different. The quote described this gentleman's life perfectly. I have used it many times since. Here is what the note said: "Life should not be a journey to the grave with the intention of arriving safely in a pretty and well-preserved body, but rather to skid in broadside in a cloud of smoke, thoroughly used up, totally worn out, and loudly proclaiming 'Wow! What a ride'" (Hunter S. Thompson). Life can be a wild ride—maybe it should be.

When I use the word *wildness*, I am not talking about the definition of wildness in its truest sense: showing a lack of discipline or restraint. Here is the picture I want you to see. When it comes to the things of the Spirit, our religious domestication prevents us from going all out. Our tendency is to hold back. Most believers have settled into a religious calm when we should be living wild in the things of the Spirit. I am not talking about living life recklessly where we put ourselves and others in harm's way. This is not what I am saying. Not willing to be a faith risk-taker is one of the main reasons we do not see the Spirit of God moving more than we do. In this last season we need to be bold risk takers: willing to step out of our comfort zones and allow the Lord to be our only comfort. Keep this in mind; you may appear foolish to most people when you step out and become wild in faith—until it starts to rain.

Even though God is speaking to his people in a loud and clear voice, many are not hearing him. Why is that? Maybe A. W. Tozer was right when he said, "Most Christians don't hear God's voice because we've already decided we aren't going to do what he says." What if we step out of our comfort zones and do what we feel the Lord wants us to do, and it all blows up in our face? Here is my counsel to you when this happens. I did not say if it happens; I said when it happens. You obey him the next time he speaks to you by stepping out and sharing the gospel with that stranger, laying your hands on someone who is sick and praying for their recovery, giving that prophetic word the Spirit gave to you for that coworker, or praying for the person you do not know in the grocery store. Can you imagine what we will begin to see and experience when we rise in our new creation identities and get wild in the things of the Spirit? This is an exciting season for the church.

UGANDA FLASHBACK—AGAIN

In our weekly pastors' meeting, we are hearing incredible things the Lord is doing in people's lives. Every week we hear about miraculous healings, divine encounters, and inexplicable moves of the Holy Spirit. Things are happening that defy rational explanation. Oftentimes, a spontaneous outburst of praise will erupt when a report is given. This is the new normal for the Lord's church, before his return.

In chapter 2, I talked briefly about our experience in Uganda. I am convinced that Uganda's story will be our story in this last-season move of God. The Spirit of God has taken me back to that life-changing moment many times over the last couple of years. I feel the Lord is saying that what we saw and experienced in Uganda will be the new normal for this season we have just entered. If that is true beloved, buckle up; we are in for a wild, glorious adventure.

From the time we arrived at the airport for our departure to Uganda, the conversation within the group was buzzing with excitement. To say that everyone's expectations were running high would be an understatement. We really believed and expected to see God do amazing things. We were not going to be disappointed. What happened during this fourteen-day period far exceeded everyone's dreams and imagination. To this day, all you must do is mention the Uganda trip to anyone who was a part of the team, and they will light up like a tiki torch. They will immediately begin to recount an experience they had on the trip.

I am convinced that what happened in Uganda will be the norm for the last-season church. It is already under way and gaining traction. It is not a season for the religiously domesticated. This is a season for those who have a wild hunger for the things of the Spirit. Things may get wild, but it will be the ride of your life.

I cannot give you a list of specifics of why we witnessed this incredible move of God in Uganda. I am not sure I know. It would be ludicrous to think that it is possible to make a "*how-to-get-God-to-move*" list. But I can give you what was shared by the team on our way back from Uganda and in posttrip meetings. The following is what I have gleaned from conversations I have had with those who participated.

Everyone was willing to step out of their comfort zones and allow the Spirit of God to do whatever he wanted to do: that included using us in ways that we had no experience, and in ways we never thought we would ever be used.

Nothing will take someone out of their comfort zone more than deliverance ministry. After all, deliverance ministry is for the professional Christian—right?

Deliverance ministry was going to be one of the top priorities on this trip. We knew from our pretrip planning meetings that witchcraft had a heavy presence in the area where we would be spending most of our time. The local leadership in Uganda had shared this information with us. Everyone on our team was familiar with deliverance ministry, but not everyone had taken someone through deliverance. Some had never sat in on a deliverance session, but they were more than willing to step out of their comfort zone so God could use them to set people free. Even though I have taken hundreds through deliverance, I had never been involved with mass deliverance with a crowd the size we were going to have. No one on the team had. I have had some hair-raising experiences in deliverance ministry, but I was not prepared for what was ahead of us. I am thankful we did not know because it could have thinned our ranks. We needed all the help we could muster.

As I have said already, we began each evening's service with a short message about salvation and what it means to be born from above. We wanted the people to know that when they accepted Jesus Christ as their Lord and Savior, they became a part of the family of God, and as a part of God's family, they have birthright privileges. Being released from one's sins is a birthright privilege, but so is freedom from any type of bondage. Once we felt this had been adequately done, we went into deliverance ministry.

This is when all comfort zones were shattered. The crowd noise increased to a level that would shatter a dog's eardrum. You could feel your heartbeat accelerate. Game was on. The experience was so overwhelming at the beginning that my first thoughts were to run. That is embarrassing for me to say, but it is the truth. I had a Jonah moment. I had my running shoes on. I was certainly a flight risk. Look out Tarshish, here I come. Reality finally smacked me in the face: Where am I going to run? A lot of water was between me and my home.

At that time in my ministry, I had taken a lot of people through deliverance. Nothing is more enjoyable than seeing someone escape from bondage. Over the years I have seen some strange and bizarre things, but nothing can compare to what was taking place in this meeting.

When people started getting set free from demonic strongholds, it increased the desire for thousands of others to seek their freedom. At one juncture in the meeting, people were stacked up like firewood in front of the stage. I do not have the words to paint this picture for you. I remember stepping on someone's face in my attempt to lay hands on an individual who was begging to be set free. It was a chaotic moment for us, but heaven was not shaken. We were experiencing a heavenly encounter.

When things settled down, a message to receive Christ as Lord and Savior was extended—again. Hundreds of hungry hearts responded to accept Christ's invitation to life. After this evangelistic appeal, we did more deliverance and prayed for people's physical healing. So many needed a healing touch from God.

When all the smoke settled and things had calmed down, an incredible peace flooded every member of the team. We knew we had just participated in a mighty move of the Spirit of God. We must have sounded like a busload of junior high school girls on their way to a homecoming dance, as we made our way back to our rooms. We could relate to how the seventy-two disciples must have felt when they returned from their evangelistic outing. "When the seventy-two disciples returned, they joyfully reported to him, 'Lord, even the demons obey us when we use your name'" (Luke 10:17 NLT). Their words could be our words. Suddenly, we found peace and rest in our new comfort zone.

This last-season movement of God is not for the tamed spectator. This is a season for the wild participator—the one who has a hunger to see and experience a powerful move of the Spirit of God; the individual who says, "I have no experience whatsoever, but here am I Lord, use me"—the child of God who will not allow a spirit of religion to intimidate them to be quiet and reserved. Like it or not—welcome to the new spiritual normal.

Not only was every member of the team willing to step out of their comfort zones and allow the Spirit of God to do whatever he wanted to do. We believed that God could perform miracles, and we were expecting a manifestation of his power and glory.

We were not disappointed. It is one thing to believe; it is another to expect. We can believe and not expect, but we cannot expect and not believe. Most Christians believe God can heal, but they do not expect him to heal. This is an issue with which most Christians wrestle, and it is what keeps us from seeing the miraculous happen on a regular basis.

Once you see and participate in a move of the Spirit of God, your faith and expectation level increases. We had an elderly man with us who kicked off all restraints, rolled up his sleeves, and jumped in with both feet. Usually when a person reaches the age of this individual, he or she is more content with the comfort of an easy chair than they are with long extended days of ministry. Every night during ministry time, he would walk deep into this huge crowd of people, leading people in receiving Christ as their Lord and Savior, praying for their healing, and setting them free from demonic bondage. Stan was a tall man, and he wore a large safari hat. This made him easily recognizable, which gave us the ability to keep an eye on him as he moved fearlessly among the people. This man believed God performed miracles, and he expected God to perform miracles. His hands of faith were filled with expectation as he laid them on the people who were crying out for help. He believed, he expected, and he saw the power and the glory of God manifest.

One of our teammates was a dear lady named Charlotte. She was an old spiritual warrior. I do not use the word *old* in a disrespectful way. This lady was a seasoned veteran in spiritual warfare. While praying for an individual, a demonic spirit said to her, "You don't know who I am." Her immediate reply was, "I know who I am, in the name of Jesus, I command you to come out—now!" Can you guess what happened? The lady that Charlotte was praying for convulsed and fell to the ground. When she regained her senses and stood up, she was a totally different person. The crowd went wild, and more people came for ministry.

Charlotte knew her identity as a child of God and because she did, the enemy could not intimidate her. The spirit that tried to frighten her got overpowered by the Spirit of God in her. She operated in faith filled with expectation. It is hard to bullyrag someone who knows who they are in Christ. Faith is, and always has been, fear's greatest nemesis.

Every night when we had our alone time as a team, we would share the experiences we had in the evening service. It was impossible for us to see what everyone was doing and experiencing because we were so engaged in ministering to a large crowd. It was a Chatty-Cathy moment. Everyone was talking at the same time, and no one was being completely heard. It was a great moment. We were all amazed that what we were believing for and expecting was happening.

This is when my understanding of the importance of believing and expecting are, to seeing God move in power. I had not realized how often I believe, but I did not expect. Believing was not my challenge; expecting was. Not expecting the miraculous to happen is the heavy weight that most of us carry that keeps us from seeing and experiencing a mighty move of the Spirit of God. This weight of no expectation needs to be cast aside during this last-season move of God if we are to be participators and not spectators.

Everyone on the team believed God could perform miracles: We also expected to see God perform miracles. There was not one spectator on the team. Everyone had a burning desire to be used by God.

Christian spectators are an alien concept to the community of faith. When the church was established, there were no spectators. Everyone was a participator. Spectators have been created over time by organized religion. We come to a nicely climatized building, dressed in our Sunday best, wearing our spiritual bibs so we can sample everything without getting it on us, from the greeting we received in the parking lot to the message preached by the pastor. We leave church with our own personal critique of the service. Church is judged by what we like instead of what our heavenly Father likes.

"I did not like that song."

"The sermon was way too long."

"They could have made the room a little warmer/cooler."

"The music was too loud—too soft.

"I do not like it when we sing all of the stanzas of a hymn."

And the consumer critique list continues. Is it any wonder we do not see a bigger move of the Spirit of God in our churches today? Church has become what we as religious consumers like instead of what God requires.

There are three kinds of people found in the church today— those who make things happen, those who watch things happen, and those who wonder what happened. There are few who make things happen; many more watch things happen, and the overwhelming majority have no idea what happened. Which group do you feel comfortable in?

If you want to participate in this last-season move of the Spirit, you must choose to be a *make-it-happen* person. If you have a burning desire to be used by God outside of your comfort zone, this becomes your only choice.

Everyone who went to Uganda had an insatiable desire to be used by God, even if it was in an area in which they had no training or experience. God loves it when a person boldly steps out and says, "God, I'm available; please use me." When this happens, God gets all the glory.

Late one night as we were returning from one of the services, the man sitting in the seat next to me was in severe pain from an abscessed tooth. His name is Fred. His wife is the one who was praying for God to show every member on the team something specific during our time in Uganda. "You wouldn't have something for a toothache, would you?" You could tell he was in pain by the way he mumbled his words. I just happened to have a tube of Orajel in my backpack. As he applied the medicine to his aching tooth, we had a brief discussion about how painful an abscessed tooth can be. Between applications he said, "There is no way that I'm going to allow a tooth to keep me from taking part in what God is doing here. This is absolutely amazing." The burning inside of Fred's heart to be used by God was greater than the burning tooth inside of his mouth. This man never pulled back or used his aching tooth as an excuse not to rise to the challenge. When you have a burning passion to be used by God, nothing can impede or stop you.

Here is the way I would describe my friend Alan. He has the mind of a scholar, the heart of a child, and the hide of a rhinoceros. What makes Alan stand out from the crowd is his burning desire to be used by God.

Alan was ministering alongside Ross, another fearless team member. They were approached by a young lady who appeared to be about thirty years old. She had been quietly observing the healings and miracles that were happening around her. This caused faith to rise inside of her. With boldness she approached both men. When she got within arm's reach, she grabbed Ross's right hand and placed it on her right eye, which was swollen to the point where it protruded past her nose. It was scaly and apparently very painful. Ross's hand was not on this lady's eye for more than ten to fifteen seconds. When he removed his hand from the infected eye, the swelling, scales, and pain were totally gone. Her right eye matched her left eye perfectly. She went from observing miracles to receiving a miracle.

This lady and her friend who had come to the crusade with her were overcome with what had just happened. They jumped, shouted, spun around, and squealed like little girls at a birthday party. Tears flowed down like a warm spring rain as they both received Jesus Christ as their Lord and Savior. The following testimony was shared with me as I was writing this chapter. It was told in our Tuesday pastors' meeting by a precious couple (Larry and Carolyn) who had recently led a three-day Encounter the Cross weekend. This ministry is focused on setting people free and keeping them free. Too many believers are alive but are not living. They may know what they have been set free from, but they do not know who they have been set free to, which is the crux of salvation. "So if the Son sets you free, you are truly free" (John 8:36 NLT). Christ does not just set us free; he really sets us free!

A lady attending the Encounter received a re-creative miracle. When she walked, she had to walk with a wide stride because there was a huge gap between her hips. Walking was a very painful experience for her. The gap between her hips was closed to a normal position after she had been prayed for. This couple who led the Encounter showed us a picture of her standing. You could not see any difference in her stance and the stance of someone who had normal hip replacement. What this couple shared with us after we saw the picture knocked us out of our chairs. The lady who received this creative miracle was a conjoined twin. She and her sister were connected at the chest and the hip at birth. They had been surgically separated, which created a large gap between her hips. There is now no gap! Testimonies like these keep coming.

Not only did everyone on the Ugandan team have an overwhelming desire to be used by God; there was singleness of vision by the team members. I am not aware of anyone who was out to make a name for themselves or to get a notch carved on the handle of their spiritual pistol. No —everyone knew that if you have more than one vision, you will end up with *di-vision*. We were in a situation where we could not afford to be distracted. The words of the Lord Jesus served as our spiritual rudder: "And I, if I am lifted up from the earth, will draw all peoples to Myself" (John 12:32 NKJV). As long as our motives were to lift the Lord high, we remained in our spiritual bubble and witnessed an incredible move of the Spirit of God.

The primary reason most moves of the Holy Spirit come to a screeching halt is because it is so easy for us humans to get distracted from the main thing. The words of Stephen Covey are worth paying attention to: "The main thing is to keep the main thing the main thing." There is nothing we can add to that.

So many ministries, churches, groups, and organizations start off with the right vision; they experience a measure of success, only to get sidetracked by forgetting why they exist. Hall of Fame Coach Vince Lombardi said, "Success demands singleness of purpose." This is true of a football team or a ministry team. Our team understood their purpose for being in Uganda—to make Jesus known and to not get in his way when he began to move. We did not try to manufacture anything. Things were kept simple. When we saw what the Lord was doing, we joined him.

We have a penchant to add to what God is doing, or to modify it so it will fit into our paradigm of how we want or think things should be. I honestly believe that most of the time we are not even aware we are doing this. The flesh is a sneaky snake. It can be very surreptitious and subtle. It can bite you before you know it is present.

LAST SEASON: THE SUPERNATURAL
BECOMES NATURAL

The church will experience miracles, signs, and wonders during this last season before the return of Christ. The supernatural will be natural for those who are daring enough to be wild about the things of the Spirit. This last-season move of the Spirit of God is a once-in-a-lifetime experience, but it is reserved for those who are willing to step out of their comfort zones.

Signs and wonders refer to experiences that are perceived to be miraculous as being normative in the modern Christian experience. Whatever you do, do not be deceived into thinking that there is a set formula for a child of God to follow that will obligate God to do anything. He is the sovereign King. We are the followers. God does not follow us and jump in when he is needed. As we follow him, we can see what he is doing, and we get to join in. The key is keep your eyes and ears open and do whatever he tells you to do no matter how foolish it may make you look. "We follow God not because we are good at following but because he is good at leading" (Johnny R. Powell).

There are things we can do, like stepping out of our comfort zones, having a desire to be used by God, and singleness of vision. This can create an atmosphere that will attract the manifest presence of God, but the final word will always be his. Be leery of anyone who can give you ten ways to get God to move; twelve steps to heaven's open door; four easy ways to see the miraculous—the list is endless. Save your money. These may sound good and even logical, but we must always remember that God is the one who is in absolute control. He is the one who sees the whole of everything. Our trust is in him. "God also bearing witness both with signs and wonders, with various miracles, and gifts of the Holy Spirit, *according to His own will*" (Hebrews 2:4 NKJV; emphasis added).

If there is one thing my experience in Uganda taught me, it is that God is still God, and what he did, he still does. God told the prophet Malachi: "For I am the Lord, I do not change" (Malachi 3:6 NKJV). Since he does not change, miracles, signs, and wonders still happen.

The season we have just entered is not a time to sit on the sidelines and watch. It is time to get wild about the things of the Spirit and participate in what God is doing. God wants you to be a part of his team. He wants to use you in ways you never dreamed were possible.

If you are a child of God, you are living in the most exciting time in human history. If you are not a child of God, this would be an excellent time to get that settled once and for all by accepting and receiving Jesus Christ as your personal Lord and Savior. You cannot go back to the beginning and do life over, but you can start right now and finish like the champion he created you to be.

We have entered the last season where the Spirit of God is draining the *church swamp*. The truth that every church is not the Lord's church, but he has his church in every church, is becoming crystal clear. The true church is being weaned off intubation. God is raising the true church out of the bed of religion and status quo. She will never again fall into a state of slumber or succumb to mediocrity. Miracles, signs, and wonders will follow those who are willing to get wild about the things of the Spirit. God is taking those of us who want to participate out of our comfort zones where we find our comfort in him and only him. The supernatural is going to be natural to those who have the audacity to believe and to those who expect it.

THE DAY OF THE LORD IS COMING

"Most importantly, I want to remind you that in the last days scoffers will come, mocking the truth and following their own desires. They will say, 'What happened to the promise that Jesus is coming again? From before the times of our ancestors, everything has remained the same since the world was first created.' They deliberately forget that God made the heavens long ago by the word of his command, and he brought the earth out from the water and surrounded it with water. Then he used the water to destroy the ancient world with a mighty flood. And by the same word, the present heavens and earth have been stored up for fire. They are being kept for the day of judgment, when ungodly people will be destroyed. But you must not forget this one thing, dear friends: A day is like a thousand years to the Lord, and a thousand years is like a day. The Lord isn't really being slow about his promise, as some people think. No, he is being patient for your sake. He does not want anyone to be destroyed but wants everyone to repent. The day of the Lord will come as unexpectedly as a thief. Then the heavens will pass away with a terrible noise, and the very elements themselves will disappear in fire, and the earth and everything on it will be found to deserve judgment. *And remember, our Lord's patience gives people time to be saved.* This is what our beloved brother Paul also wrote to you with the wisdom God gave him" (2 Peter 3:3–10, 15 NLT; emphasis added).

We should live as if Christ died yesterday—arose today—and is coming back tomorrow.

IMMUNITY FROM
SPIRITUAL COVID

We've heard a lot over the last few years about vaccines that are available with the promise they will help keep people from contracting COVID. Even though these vaccines were not validated by testing that comes from time, we were assured they were failproof. At one point, we were told that these vaccines were so effective in building immunity against this horrible disease that there was an attempt to mandate that people must take these shots or pay the consequences. And pay we have. Time has proven that a considerable amount of the information we were given was not accurate. Yes, these vaccines did and do help in many instances. What we have not been given are the numbers of people (ranging in the millions) who fought COVID many times even though they had been fully vaccinated. And most of them had taken all the boosters as well.

By no means am I antivaccine or against taking the COVID shots or any other vaccines. I am not downplaying the reality of COVID. My wife and I had to deal with this horrible virus that invaded our bodies. It was not a pleasant experience for either of us. The point I want to make is that man-made vaccines cannot guarantee 100 percent that a person's immune system can be boosted to the point where their bodies will be totally protected from catching an illness. It's just not going to happen.

This book, *Spiritual COVID*, is not about a physical virus. Discussing that subject with any reasonable intelligence is outside the parameters of my expertise. I'll leave that to reputable immunologists. I am addressing the spiritual virus that has infiltrated and affected the community of faith—the body of Christ. It has proven to be very contagious and debilitating. This virus was created in the demonic laboratories in the pit of hell and was released on humanity dating as far back as the third chapter of the book of Genesis. This deadly sin virus corrupted the seed of humankind in the very beginning of time and has been passed on for millenniums to every person who has been born. In this last season of time, it seems to have gained momentum. We have a spiritual COVID pandemic on our hands. The body of Christ is sick and needs to be treated and immunized from this deadly disease. It has brought untold harm and damage to the body of Christ, and it is time for the community of faith to rise and say that enough is enough.

THE SIN VIRUS

I'm going to suggest that you go back and read the first chapter again where we discussed the six symptoms of the spiritual COVID syndrome: doing over being, human ability over anointing, personality over character, talent over spiritual gifting, positive thinking over faith, and human opinion over God's word. I have branded these as the six symptoms that indicate the presence of a deeper and more dangerous problem—spiritual COVID.

Here is the good news. A vaccine is available that has the power to immunize an individual from contracting spiritual COVID. And one pill is all it takes to protect us from this deadly spiritual disease—*the gos-pill*. Its effectiveness against sin-sickness was proven to be trustworthy before time ever began. It is the blood of the perfect Lamb of God—Jesus. "And all the people who belong to this world worshiped the beast. They are the ones whose names were not written in the Book of Life that belongs to *the Lamb who was slaughtered before the world was made*" (Revelation 13:8 NLT; emphasis added). Once again, we see how God took care of fallen humanity's problems outside of time before there was ever a problem in time. Christ shedding his blood on the cross to give every person the opportunity to be reconciled with God was not an afterthought. This was God's plan long before He began the beginning of time.

The blood of Jesus inoculates us from contracting spiritual COVD and any of its variants. That is incredible news because sin has many manifestations. What we need to grab a hold of is the difference between sin and sins. The sin that separates a person from God for eternity is the sin of "unbelief." Sins, plural, are the fruits of unbelief. In keeping with the proposition of this book, we could say that sins are the variants of sin. We do what we do because of what we believe. If we believe wrong, it won't be long until we behave wrong. Unbelief is deadly. It is a spiritual virus that can only be effectively treated by the blood of Jesus.

The enemy has convinced us that the most important thing we can do to be good Christians is to manage the fruits in our lives that are produced by a corrupt root. Once again, the sin of unbelief is what spawns behavior that is unbecoming for a child of God. Until we become resolute in dealing with the root of unbelief, we will continue to battle spiritual COVID. There is only one outcome— we lose. If we take care of the root of unbelief, we will spend less time, energy, and resources dealing with the fruits it produces. If we don't, we will find ourselves consumed by a recycling ministry of rededication. This makes it impossible for us to enjoy the peace and freedom that comes from our new creation identities because we are so busy dealing with our missteps—our out-of-character behavior. Never forget, whatever we choose to focus on is what we will default to. There are no exceptions. "Since you have been *raised to new life* with Christ, *set your sights on the realities of heaven*, where Christ sits in the place of honor at God's right hand. *Think about the things of heaven, not the things of the earth.* For you died to this life, and *your real life is hidden with Christ in God.* And when Christ, *who is your life*, is revealed to the whole world, you will share in all his glory" (Colossians 3:1–4 NLT; emphasis added).

IMMUNITY AGAINST SPIRITUAL COVID

Immunity is the condition of being able to resist a particular disease especially through preventing development of pathogenic microorganism or by counteracting the effects of its product. The immune system is what protects our bodies from diseases and infections. If we have a compromised immune system, we become susceptible to serious illnesses, which can have deadly consequences.

I am fully aware that my weak and immature commentary on the three types of immunities will not be published in the *New England Journal of Medicine*, or any medical journal, but I see a correlation between physical immunity and spiritual immunity.

When we use the word *immunity*, we are talking about the immune system's way of protecting the body against an infectious disease. It is the ability of the human body to defend itself against disease-causing organisms. There are three types of immunity: innate, adaptive, and passive. Let me briefly define the three.

Innate immunity is present in us at birth. It will be in us for our entire lifetime. Innate immunity is the first response against an invading infection. It is also referred to as natural immunity.

Let's shift our thoughts from innate immunity that we received at our physical birth to innate spiritual immunity we received when we were born again. Immunity against sin (unbelief) and all its variants (actions) was provided for us when we had our second birth date. This is why Jesus said to Nicodemus, "Most assuredly I say to you, unless one is born again [born from above], he cannot see the kingdom of God" (John 3:3 NKJV; emphasis added). The moment we were born again, the blood of Jesus inoculated us from the sin of unbelief and all the consequences of that sin. There is no need for a booster shot because the Holy Spirit took up residence in us at the moment of our confession. Our sins of the past, present, and future have been expiated by the blood of Jesus. All our sin-guilt was extinguished the moment we said yes to God's invitation to life, a life that is only available through his son Jesus Christ.

Then, there is adaptive immunity. Adaptive immunity occurs in response to being infected with or vaccinated against a microorganism. It is also known as the acquired immune system. The same is true in the spiritual realm. We acquired the righteousness of Jesus Christ by faith, not by our works. "Grace and peace be multiplied to you in the knowledge of God and of Jesus our Lord, as His divine power has given to us all things that pertain to life and godliness, through the knowledge of Him who called us by glory and virtue, by which have been given to us exceedingly great and precious promises, that through these you may be *partakers of the divine nature*, having escaped the corruption that is in the world thorough lust" (2 Peter 1:2–4 NKJV; emphasis added). When you received Jesus Christ as your Lord and Savior, his righteousness was imparted to you at that moment.

Last but not least is passive immunity. Passive immunity occurs when we are protected from a pathogen by immunity gained from someone else. A newborn baby acquires passive immunity from its mother through the placenta. A baby does nothing to receive it. It was imparted at birth—it is a gift. All believers have gained resistance to spiritual COVID without having to actively do anything to get it. It was imparted to us when we were born from above. Physical immunity will last for a brief period, but spiritual immunity will last for eternity.

Now, let's use these three physical immunities to paint a picture of what being inoculated against spiritual COVID with the blood of Jesus and the word of God looks like. Both have been tested by time and have never failed. Never! Here is some fantastic news: They will never fail to inoculate those who have accepted and received Jesus Christ as their Lord and Savior. When a person is born from above (born again), he or she has had a second birth date, which gives them innate immunity against spiritual COVID. It is not natural immunity that comes from one's physical birth. It is God's gift to you at the moment of your spiritual birth experience. It is supernatural immunity because it comes from being born of the Spirit (John 3:1–8 NKJV).

Let me repeat what I just said. Only two things have the power to protect a person from spiritual COVD, and that is the blood of Jesus and the word of God. The blood heals us from spiritual COVID, and living in the word keeps our spiritual immune system fully boosted.

IMMUNIZED BY THE BLOOD OF JESUS

The blood of Jesus is the only vaccine that can protect us (the body of Christ) from contracting spiritual COVID. We're not talking about a drug. We're talking about blood; and it is not just any blood. It is the blood that Jesus shed at the whipping post and on an old, rugged cross for the remission of our sin(s). Our sin record was expunged by his blood for eternity. This might be a good time to shout! If you don't feel like it, I will shout for you.

The first testimony of blood is found in the book of Genesis when Cain committed the first murder. He killed his brother, Able. God asked Cain this question: "But the Lord said, 'What have you done? Listen! *Your brother's blood cries out to me* from the ground'" (Genesis 4:10 NLT; emphasis added)! Cain shed his brother's blood, and God heard it crying out from the ground. Blood has a voice, and God hears it.

Before Cain committed the first murder by taking his brother's life, there seems to have been another instance of the shedding of blood; at least it has the appearance there was. "And the Lord *God made clothing from animal* skins for Adam and his wife" (Genesis 3:21 NLT). Where did these skins come from? That is a logical and appropriate question to ask. We know that God could have spoken these skins into existence without the shedding of blood in the same way that he spoke all of creation into being. All he had to do was say the word, and things that had never existed before appeared. We must not overlook that possibility. On the other hand, could it be that God shed the first blood to get the skins to cover Adam and Eve's sin? These skins did not remove their sin. Their sin of unbelief was covered. I am convinced that God was setting the stage for how he would deal with sin under the old covenant. An individual's sin would be covered by the sacrificing of an animal. This is the introduction of the sin of unbelief that we talked about in the beginning of this chapter.

Adam and Eve did what God told them not to do. They ate from the forbidden tree, the tree of the knowledge of good and evil (Genesis 3:16–17 NKJV). They did not believe what God told them would happen if they ate from that tree. Their sin of unbelief gave life to death and then death took their lives. Sin, with all its variants, entered humans. This sin gene was passed on to their offspring and to all of humanity (Romans 3:9–20 NKJV). We could say that spiritual COVID was given life by disobedience—not believing what God said. This deadly sin virus would require a medicament that would not only treat spiritual COVID but keep it from being passed on to others. This is something that can only be done by the blood of Jesus.

Thank God we are under a new covenant. When we confessed Jesus as our Lord and Savior—the Lamb of God—our sins were not covered. They were taken away forever, not to be remembered against us anymore. There is a song the church has sung for years. Robert Lowry wrote it in 1876. The title of this song is "What Can Wash Away My Sin."

What can wash away my sin?
Nothing but the blood of Jesus;
What can make me whole again?
Nothing but the blood of Jesus.

Oh! precious is the flow
That makes me white as snow;
No other fount I know,
Nothing but the blood of Jesus.

For my pardon, this I see,
Nothing but the blood of Jesus;
For my cleansing this my plea,
Nothing but the blood of Jesus.

Nothing can for sin atone,
Nothing but the blood of Jesus;
Naught of good that I have done,
Nothing but the blood of Jesus.

This is all my hope and peace,
Nothing but the blood of Jesus;
This is all my righteousness,
Nothing but the blood of Jesus.

Now by this I'll overcome—
Nothing but the blood of Jesus;
Now by this I'll reach my home—
Nothing but the blood of Jesus.

Glory! Glory! This I sing—
Nothing but the blood of Jesus,
All my praise for this I bring—
Nothing but the blood of Jesus.

Nothing but the blood. We must never underestimate the power of the blood. Under the new covenant, our sins are not covered by a sacrificial offering of an animal. They are removed by the blood of Jesus—the perfect Lamb of God. "For the law, having a shadow of the good things to come, and not the very image of the things, *can never with these same sacrifices*, which they offer continually year by year, make those who approach perfect. For then would they not have ceased to be offered. For the worshipers, once purified, would have had no more consciousness of sins. But in those sacrifices, there is a reminder of sins every year. *For it is not possible that the blood of bulls and goats could take away sins* (Hebrews 9:1–4 NKJV; emphasis added). That was the old covenant.

Under the new covenant our sins were removed as far as the east is from the west by the precious blood of the Lamb of God (Jesus). The blood of Jesus Christ cleanses us from all sin (1 John 1:7 NKJV). The precious blood of the Lamb released us from the curse that had been placed on all of humanity because of the sin of unbelief by Adam and his covenant partner, Eve. This is when spiritual COVID was released on the entire human race and has been rampant ever since. The only way it can be effectively treated and destroyed is by a blood transfusion. What can wash away our sins is nothing but the blood of Jesus.

IMMUNIZED BY THE WORD OF GOD

By faith we accept the word of God as our standard for living our lives. It is the plumb bob that keeps our lives square, in order, balanced, and healthy. We must resist all attempts by people who try to pervert the scriptures or cast doubt about them. The word of God is absolute truth. That means it can never be altered or dismissed as being irrelevant. There is no such thing as woke scriptures. If we deny and compromise God's word, we become susceptible to all sorts of spiritual COVID variants.

We are hearing a lot of rhetoric today that is diametrically opposed to the word of God. Because most Christians do very little personal study of the Bible on their own, they are susceptible to being carried away by every wind of doctrine. Paul warned the church in Ephesus about the danger of being deceived and led astray by those who have challenged the word of God as being infallible. "Now these are the gifts Christ gave to the church: the apostles, the prophets, the evangelists, and the pastors and teachers. Their responsibility is to equip God's people to do his work and build up the church, the body of Christ. This will continue until we all come to such unity in our faith and knowledge of God's Son that we will be mature in the Lord, measuring up to the full and complete standard of Christ. Then we will no longer be immature like children. *We won't be tossed and blown about by every wind of new teaching. We will not be influenced when people try to trick us with lies so clever, they sound like the truth* (Ephesians 4:11–14 NLT; emphasis added). For many years, the church has ignored this admonition given by Paul and is now paying the price for not obeying.

"Every part of Scripture is God-breathed and useful one way or another—showing us truth, exposing our rebellion, correcting our mistakes, training us to live God's way. Through the Word we are put together and shaped up for the tasks God has for us" (2 Timothy 3:16 TPT). If this verse is true, and I'm convinced it is, then the enemy has no choice but to try and cast doubt on its legitimacy, because truth is his kryptonite. He is a liar and has no defense against the truth (John 8:44 NKJV). Here is a snippet from the prayer Jesus prayed for his disciples, and for you and me. "Sanctify them by Your truth. Your word is truth" (John 17:17 NKJV). If the devil can cast doubt on the authenticity of the scriptures, he can cause people to doubt the deity of Jesus. If the scriptures are not true, then Jesus was nothing more than a fraud and a con artist.

No other book has been so savagely attacked, assaulted, and ridiculed like the Bible. I'm convinced the devil knows his time is rapidly coming to an end, so he has no choice but to pull out all the stops. He is acutely aware that he is fighting a fight that he has already lost, so he wants to take down as many people with him as possible. He has no doubt about the word of God being the truth. He also knows that if God's people make their home in the scriptures, he will lose all his influence over them. They will never suffer from spiritual COVID, because the word of God inoculates them from believing his lies about the authenticity and infallibility of the scriptures. The devil is completely aware that the written word is the very breathe of God—every part of scripture is God-breathed. "Then Jesus said to those Jews who believed Him, 'If you abide in My word, you are My disciples indeed. And you shall know the truth, and the truth shall make you free'" (John 8:31–32 NKJV). Read those two verses again. It does not say truth sets you free. Jesus said the truth you know from living (abiding) in his word not only sets you free; the truth found in his word will keep you free. This is why the enemy will do everything within his power to distract us from spending time in the word of God. Again, he knows the scriptures are true, and if the people of God will make their home there, they are inoculated against spiritual COVID and all its variants. "Therefore, if the Son [Jesus] makes you free, you shall be free indeed" (John 8:36 NKJV).

EARLY WARNING SIGNS FOR SPIRITUAL COVID

Medical academia has given us some emergency warning signs that a person may be catching COVID. They are as follows:

- trouble breathing;
- persistent pain or pressure in the chest;
- new confusion;
- inability to wake or stay awake;
- pale, gray, or blue-colored skin, lips, or nail beds, depending on skin tone.

There are other warning signs, but these are the potentially life-threatening ones. It is highly recommended that if a person is experiencing any of these symptoms, he or she should seek emergency care as quickly as possible. Neglecting them could be costly.

In chapter 1 I talked about symptoms that might be present if a believer is or has been exposed to spiritual COVID. If these symptoms are left untreated, they can lead to full-blown spiritual COVID. There are also some warning signs that a person may have been exposed to spiritual COVID. They are as follows:

- we begin to judge the truth based on our experiences,
- we begin to replace spiritual things with material things,
- we begin to disengage from the community of faith,
- we begin to lose the joy of worship and,
- we begin to question the integrity of the scriptures.

There are other warning signs, but if these that I have given are ignored, we might find ourselves doing things that we said we would never do, going places we said we would never go, and saying things we thought we would never say.

WE BEGIN TO JUDGE THE TRUTH BASED ON OUR EXPERIENCES

No one is denying that experiences are not real. The question is are they true. We should always demand that our experiences rise to the level of truth and not dumb down the truth to validate our experiences. You can always tell when someone has reached this point by what they say. "I know what the word of God says, but—." Whatever a person says after the conjunction *but* is what they really believe. Their validation of truth is based on experiences instead of allowing the word of God, which is truth, to validate their experiences.

Our feelings are what really get in the way. Because feelings are real, we assume they are true. This is not necessarily true. I may feel God does not love me, and those feelings are real, but the truth is, he does. Nothing I can do will ever cause him to not love me. We take a huge step forward in our spiritual maturation process when we understand that feelings are not fundamental to faith.

I hear people say all the time that the reason they don't pray is because they don't feel like it. If we pray when we don't feel like it, then we are hypocrites, and God won't answer our prayers. This is the position of most believers. This is true in other areas of our lives as well: Attending church, giving, witnessing, the list is endless. If this is true in your life, you are experiencing a warning sign that you may be contracting spiritual COVID. If ignored, the battle for our spiritual health will intensify and cause irreparable harm. When our experiences carry more weight and authority than does the word of God, we may need to be intubated so we can be effectively treated. A lot of Christians have been placed on life support, and they are not even aware of it.

WE BEGIN TO REPLACE SPIRITUAL THINGS WITH MATERIAL THINGS

When we put more stock in our experiences than we do truth, it's only a matter of time before we begin to replace spiritual things with material things. This transition can be so subtle that we are not even aware of it. The enemy of our souls knows that if he can get us to shift our focus off Christ and onto ourselves, he gets a stronger toehold in dictating how we live. The material world becomes more important to us than the spiritual realm. Paul addressed this issue with the church at Rome. *"Don't copy the behavior and customs of this world,* but let God transform you into a new person by changing the way you think. Then you will learn to know God's will for you, which is good and pleasing and perfect"* (Romans 12:2 NLT;

emphasis added). Do not allow the world to form, shape, or fashion you into something you are not. You are a new creation in Christ, and it is high time for us to start living like it.

It is imperative that we do not ignore this warning sign. It can compromise and even destroy our spiritual health. This does not mean that Christians should not have material possessions. We need to make sure that material things don't have us.

WE BEGIN TO DISENGAGE FROM THE COMMUNITY OF FAITH

Disengagement is another warning sign that our spiritual health is under attack by a spiritual virus. We were created for community, and to neglect that gives the enemy more control of our lives. If this does happen, we will easily become self-centered, which makes us vulnerable to criticism, which will lead to us walking away from engaging with the family of faith. If you know someone who at one time was faithful, but they have fallen away, more than likely this is what happened. They got their feelings hurt, and instead of going to their knees, they stayed on their feet and walked away. I have seen this happen time and time again in my fifty-years as a pastor. It would be impossible for me to count how many times I've heard these words spoken by children of God: "So-and-so said this about me," and then they will usually tell you what was said. They end up leaving the fellowship of believers because they got their feelings hurt. What they are really saying, is "I've focused my attention more on people than I have God." When we choose to make others more important than the Lord, we expose ourselves to all kinds of invasions by the enemy.

The community of faith is filled with spiritual vagabonds. They roam from church to church looking for, but never finding, a home. Like West Texas tumbleweeds, they are constantly being blown around by every wind of doctrine. And all it takes is a shift of focus, from Christ to people. "And let us not neglect our meeting together, as some people do, but encourage one another, especially now that the day of his return is drawing near" (Hebrews 10:25 NLT). Need we say more?

WE BEGIN TO LOSE THE JOY OF WORSHIP

Another serious warning sign that we need to be alert to is losing the joy of worship. For a Christian, worship is the glue that holds everything together. It keeps us focused on the main thing, and that is the Lord Jesus Christ. If being entertained by worship becomes more important to us than worship, we will find ourselves on a slippery slope. I'm afraid performance has replaced true worship in many places. Worship is the key to staying sane in a world that has gone insane. True worship is not about singing a three-to-four-song set that we participate in with other believers in a church service. Because we do not have a healthy understanding of what worship truly is, we hear things like this said:

"Now that worship is over, we will share with you a message from the word of God."

"I really enjoyed the message today, but I was not impressed with the worship service." We all have heard things just like this. We may have even said it. Worship is not a style of living; it is a lifestyle.

The writer of Hebrews gives us some insight into what worship is and what it is not. We are also given where worship ranks among what I call the big three—worship, walk, and work. It is so important that we have things in biblical order. If we ever get these out of sequence, and I'm convinced we certainly have, our spiritual lives will grind like a motor needing oil. Worshipping God, walking with God, and working with God are crucial to good spiritual health, and the word of God tells us what order they should be in. If worship is not our top priority, we are setting ourselves up to be exposed to the spiritual COVID virus and all its variants.

Before we peek at what the book of Hebrews says about the big three, let's see what Jesus says our number one priority should be. In Luke 10:38–42 we find Jesus in the home of two sisters, Martha and Mary. Martha was working in the kitchen while Mary was sitting at the feet of Jesus. One sister was serving, and the other one was sitting. "But Martha was distracted with much serving, and she approached Him and said 'Lord, do you not care that my sister has left me to serve alone?' Therefore, tell her to help me" (Luke 10:40 NKJV). Once again, don't lose sight of this: Martha was working while Mary was worshiping. Here's what Jesus told Martha: "And Jesus answered and said to her, 'Martha, Martha, you are worried and troubled about many things. *But one thing is needed, and Mary has chosen that good part, which will not be taken away from her*" (Luke 10:41–42 NKJV; emphasis added). Jesus sets the record straight about worship—Mary had chosen the good part. Work has supplanted worship in the body of Christ for the most part. The number one priority for you and me is worship. When the worship of our Lord and Savior Jesus Christ becomes our number one priority, everything else will fall into place. Now let's take a quick glance at that Hebrews passage I mentioned earlier.

Hebrews chapter 11 is often called the Hall of Faith. The "big names" of the faith are mentioned; people like Abraham, his wife Sarah, Isaac, Jacob, Joseph, Moses, and the list of heavyweights in the faith continues. But oftentimes not much attention is given to the first three names recorded in this chapter on faith. They are Abel, Enoch, and Noah. Each of these men represents one of the three aspects of the Christian life that must be in its proper place and order. Worship—Walk—Work.

Let's be sincerely honest with ourselves. Of these three, what would you say the primary focus of the church is on today? I think you nailed it on the head if you said working for God. We cannot and must never underestimate the importance of our participation in kingdom work. There is an abundant shortage of dedicated and sacrificial workers in the body of Christ today. Almost every aspect of the church has posted "now hiring" signs. Very few applications are being submitted. Diligent work is to be commended, but we should never allow it to replace our worship of the Lord. If we do, we will have things out of order, and it is only a matter of time before everything goes south.

ABEL WORSHIPPED GOD

"By faith *Abel offered to God a more excellent sacrifice* than Cain, through which he obtained witness that he was righteous, God testifying of *his gifts*; and through it he being dead still speaks" (Hebrews 11:4 NKJV; emphasis added). Able offered to God a more excellent sacrifice than his brother—worship. The first person listed in this incredible chapter of Hebrews is a man whose priority was putting God first in his life. That's what worship is. It's more than singing a few hymns or praise songs in a quote, unquote worship service. The most prominent word used for worship in the New Testament scriptures is the Greek word *Proskuneo*, meaning to kiss. If you can get this picture indelibly engraved in your mind, you will never forget what worship is. Think about a loving dog coming up to its master in total submission and begins to softly, and lovingly, lick the back of their hand. This is what worship looks like. Worship is a lifestyle (a life totally surrendered to God), not a style of worship. We will not worship someone we do not love.

ENOCH WALKED WITH GOD

"By faith Enoch was taken away so that *he did not see death, and was not found, because God* had taken him, for before he was taken had this testimony, that he pleased God" (Hebrews 11:5 NKJV; emphasis added). Genesis tells us that Enoch lived 365 years, and he walked with God three hundred of those years (Genesis 5:22–23 NKJV).

The prophet Amos may be considered one of the twelve minor prophets in the Old Testament, but he wrote something not-so-minor in the short book that bears his name about walking in agreement with someone. "Do two people walk hand in hand if they aren't going to the same place?" (Amos 3:3 TPT).

Let me give you a simple illustration that I believe will give insight into what it means to walk in agreement with the Lord. Let's say the Lord told us that our walking together would require that we go west. Instead of going with Him, we decide to go the opposite direction, east. If we say that we are walking *with* God, yet we are traveling in the opposite direction that He told us we must go, we are living in deception. To *walk with Him* means we are holding His hand and wherever He goes, we go. How do we know what direction our Lord is going? His word is our map, and the Holy Spirit is our GPS. We will not walk with someone we do not agree with.

NOAH WORKED FOR GOD

"By faith Noah, being divinely warned of things not yet seen, moved with godly fear, prepared an ark for the saving of his household, by which he condemned the world and became heir of the righteousness which is according to faith" (Hebrews 11:7 NKJV). You don't mind working for someone you agree with. And you do not mind worshipping the one you love. With all the ridicule and mockery that Noah was subjected to, he remained faithful to the assignment God had given him—building the ark. People could not persuade Noah to give up his building project because his trust was in God. "Noah found favor in the eyes of the Lord" (Genesis 6:8 NKJV). Even though the construction of the ark took a considerable amount of time, Noah never quit on the Lord.

When we keep things in their proper order, no one or nothing can cause us to surrender. Making the Lord our number one priority keeps the door to worship wide open. We will always have a burning desire deep within our souls to spend time with Him: Nothing else can take its place. Walking and working with the Lord will be something that we want to do, not something we have to do. We will not work for someone we do not love and trust.

WE BEGIN TO QUESTION THE INTEGRITY OF THE SCRIPTURES

There is one more warning sign that we must never overlook or scuff off as not being important. This one may give the appearance of being benign, but it is crafty and very deadly. It has the power to metastasize rapidly if it ever gets its tentacles wrapped around a person's mind. The person may never recover if he or she chooses to ignore it. Because this spiritual COVID warning sign is so virulent, we will spend the next chapter dealing with it: questioning the integrity of the scriptures. Downplaying or overlooking this warning sign can be lethal to one's spiritual health.

THE MOST
DANGEROUS
WARNING SIGN
OF ALL

M any people are interrupting the word of God today in a way that resembles the sign one might find over a blacksmith's shop: Bending and Twisting Done Here. Human nature has the tendency to bend and twist the scriptures to support one's belief system; especially if the word of God condemns the way people have chosen to live their lives. If you take a close look at a person's Bible, you will find that most (if not all) of the scriptures they have underlined or highlighted are the ones they agree with. If you do not believe this, why don't you take a gander at your own Bible.

This would be a good time to repeat something that I've already said because it is so crucial in keeping us from becoming a victim of Satan's diabolic scheme—and that is to sully the apple of God's eyes—all of humanity. It is never the *will* of God if it goes against the *word* of God. Never!

If we ever reach the point where we begin to feel uncertain about any part of the Word of God, it creates an untenable theological hermeneutic of the entire scriptures. If we begin to doubt any portion of the scriptures, it won't be long until we call into question the truth of others. We believe it all, or we don't believe it at all.

Being suspicious of the integrity of the scriptures will move people to what they feel and believe rather than what the word of God says. It is a slippery slope. All the enemy needs to wreak havoc in our lives is for us to bring into question any part of the word of God. And it doesn't take much. It is like getting a microspeck of a foreign substance on your contact lenses. It does not take much to create pain and panic. And all contact lens wearers said—Amen! If we become suspicious of what the word of God says, we are falling into a trap that very few people ever escape from. This variant of spiritual COVID is lurking in the shadows of every person's life looking for opportunities to gain entrance. The way to stay safe is to never open the door when doubt comes knocking. The holy scriptures are the inspired, infallible, inerrant word of God regardless of whether a person believes them to be or not.

SEEDS OF REBELLION WERE FIRST PLANTED IN HEAVEN

Where did doubt and distrust concerning the word of God begin? Most people will probably say that it began in the third chapter of the book of Genesis. I certainly would not dispute that answer. That is certainly the time and place where the DNA of doubt concerning the word of God was planted in the hearts and minds of Adam and Eve. We will look at that in a moment. But the truth is, challenging the authority of the word of God began long before there was ever a world inhabited by people.

In the Old Testament book that bears the prophet Isaiah's name, God is reading Satan's mind like a cheap novel. As you read this portion of the scriptures mediate on this: There is a name for the person who wants to go toe-to-toe with the Creator of this universe and everything in it: victim!

"*You said to yourself,* 'I'll climb to heaven. I'll set my throne over the stars of God. I'll run the assembly of angels that meets on sacred Mount Zaphon. I'll climb to the top of the clouds. I'll take over as King of the Universe'" (Isaiah 14:12–14 TPT; emphasis added). Even though Satan was talking to himself, God heard every word he muttered. "I will climb"; "I will establish my throne"; "I will run things"; "I will ascend to the top of the clouds"; "I will take over as King."

This is nothing more than an attempted angelic coup to take over the government of heaven. This attempt at unlawful seizure of power began when Satan challenged the authority of God. He sealed his own fate by thinking he could override whatever God said. He forgot one very important thing—God says what he means and means what he says. "I am God, the only God there is. Besides me there are no real gods" (Isaiah 45:5 TPT). Satan's attempt at a coup d'état did not turn out so well for him, along with the angelic hosts who sided with him.

God allowed the devil to shinny up the tree of pride so he could saw the limb out from under him. I love what God says to this minion after his rant. You can hear God's chainsaw cranking up. "But you didn't make it, did you? Instead of climbing up, you came down—down with the underground dead, down to the abyss of the pit. People will stare and muse: 'Can this be the one Who terrorized earth and its kingdoms, turned earth to a moonscape, wasted its cities, shut up his prisoners to a living death?'" (Isaiah 14:15–17 TPT). God may give you some wiggle room to talk, but you can be assured of one thing; he will always have the last word.

THE DEMONIC COUP MOVES
FROM HEAVEN TO EARTH

The devil was unsuccessful in his attempted takeover of the heavenly realm, so he thought he would give it another try in the earthly realm. His rebellion got him kicked out of heaven along with all his imps. This brings us to Genesis chapter 3.

"Now the serpent was the shrewdest of all the wild animals the Lord God had made. One day he asked the woman, '*Did God really say* you must not eat the fruit from any of the trees in the garden?'" (Genesis 3:1 NLT; emphasis added). At first read, this does not seem to be a baited question. But it is frothed with poison. The devil is chumming the waters to see if he can get Adam and Eve to take a bite of his deception.

"Did God really say?" Well, what did God say? "The Lord God placed the man in the Garden of Eden to tend and watch over it. But the Lord God warned him, 'You may freely eat the fruit of every tree in the garden—*except the tree of the knowledge of good and evil. If you eat its fruit, you are sure to die*'" (Genesis 2:15–17 NLT, emphasis added). It does not sound like God was ambiguous in his warning about eating from the forbidden tree. If they chose to disobey, it would lead to their spiritual deaths and physical expulsion from the Garden of Eden.

THREE TACTICS THE ENEMY USES TO SPREAD SPIRITUAL COVID

The first tactic the devil used on Eve in his attempt to cast doubt on what God had told her about eating fruit form the tree of the knowledge of good and evil was by benignly confronting the validity of what God said: "Did God really say?" The serpent knew that if he could plant a seed of doubt in Eve's mind, it would enhance his chances of taking control of her entire life. One seed of doubt has the potential to metastasize into full-blown spiritual COVID.

The serpent is very skilled at confronting the truth about the penalty that is meted out to the ones who begin to question the integrity of the word of God. He also knew that if he could sucker Adam and Eve with this seemingly innocent question ("Has God really said?"), it would be much easier for him to lead them astray. This is why doubting the validity of the word of God is the most dangerous warning sign that spiritual COVID is prowling around seeking someone to devour. If this goes unnoticed and untreated, it will lead to a sure death.

We are flirting with big trouble when we begin to embrace and accept what God says is wrong, or at least questionable. We will start looking for what appears to be contradictions in the holy scriptures. Let me say something about the appearance of contradictions in the word of God before we move on with exposing Satan's tactics to deceive humanity by calling into question the absolute, unadulterated truth of what God says.

In Paul's letter to the Colossian church, he writes: "For in Him (Jesus) dwells all the fullness of the Godhead bodily; and *you are complete in Him*, who is the head of all principality and power" (Colossians 2:9–10 NKJV; emphasis added). The scriptures clearly state that a believer finds completion in Christ and Christ alone. "You (we) are complete in Him." We are made whole in Jesus? If that is true, then how do we square that with what Paul writes to the Philippian church? "Being confident of this very thing, that *He who has begun a good work in you will complete it* until the day of Jesus Christ" (Philippians 1:6 NKJV). It doesn't take a rocket scientist to recognize what appears to be a contradiction between these two verses. Are we complete in Christ, or are we being made complete? This is a legitimate question that begs for an answer. Some of the best teaching that I've ever heard when it comes to hermeneutics (Bible interpretation), is this: when you find what appears to be a contradiction in the scriptures, this is exactly what you have—an appearance.

Let me give you the answer to this question: "Are we now complete in Christ, or are we in the process of being made complete," so we can move on with exposing the devil's scheme to get believers to become suspicious that the word of God may not be inspired (God as the definitive author), inerrant (without mixture of error), or infallible (incapable of error).

In the unseen realm (spiritual) we are complete because we are in Christ (Ephesians 2:4–6 NKJV). In the seen realm (natural) we are being made complete. Let me put it this way: In this earthly realm we are in the process of becoming what we already are in the heavenly realm. If that won't make you shout, your shouter is broke. As my brother would say, "If that doesn't ring your bell, your clapper is broke."

I love what Paul said to the church in Rome about what happens when man's opinion tries to override what God says: "Of course not! Even if everyone else is a liar, God is true. As the Scriptures say about him, *'You will be proved right in what you say*, and you will win your case in court'" (Romans 3:4 NLT; emphasis added).

"Has God indeed said, 'You shall not eat of every tree of the garden?'" (Genesis 3:1 NKJV). As I stated earlier, on the surface this question seems to be just small talk—no big deal. But it was more than that. It was Satan's attempt to expose Adam and Eve to the spiritual COVID virus. Confrontation of truth (the most dangerous of all warning signs) is the first phase of contracting full-blown spiritual COVID.

The second tactic the serpent used against Adam and Eve was to conceal the truth about the consequences that come from not accepting God's word as absolute truth. "For God knows that in *the day you eat* of it your eyes will be opened, and you will be like God, knowing good and evil" (Genesis 3:5 NKJV; emphasis added). There are two incredible truths in this verse that must not be overlooked. First, Adam and Eve were already like God (Genesis 1:26–27 NKJV). If they chose to ignore what God told them not to do, their true identities will be stolen. What Satan concealed from Eve was what happened to him in heaven when he went against the authority of God. He was removed from the presence of God. His disobedience got him kicked out of heaven, and he knew the same fate awaits Adam and Eve if they choose to disobey God's word. They would be removed from the Garden of Eden; they could no longer live in intimate fellowship with their Creator.

The enemy knows the power of truth because truth is what exposes his lies (John 8:44 NKJV). If an individual embraces the truth (the word of God), not only will he or she be free, that person will remain free (John 8:36 NKJV). The serpent has no defense against truth. This is why he is so dedicated in his attempts to confront and conceal the truth about the word of God.

This would be a good time to ask the question, What is truth? Simply stated, truth is whatever God says: case closed. Jesus (who is the Living Word) defines truth for us in John's Gospel account. "I do not pray that You should take them out of the world, but that You should keep them from the evil one. They are not of the world, just as I am not of the world. *Sanctify them by Your truth. Your word is truth*" (John 17:15–17 NKJV; emphasis added). Not only is Jesus praying for his followers then; his prayer is for his followers today. Just think about how good this is: Jesus prayed for you before he went to the cross. He clearly says that if we take our stand on the word of God, we will be standing on truth. I know this makes you want to run around and shout, so, go for it!

Knowing the truth does not come easily, nor is it obtained without effort on our parts. Once again, let's listen to the Living Word (Jesus) tell us how truth is acquired. "Then Jesus said to those Jews who believed in Him, '*if you abide in My word*, you are My disciples indeed. *And you shall know the truth, and the truth shall make you free*'" (John 8:31–32 NKJV; emphasis added). Sometimes it is good to pay attention to what a verse does not say to see what it really says. Jesus did not say that truth sets us free. Truth is truth whether we are free or not. Freedom comes from the truth we know. The word *know* is a word of intimacy. Knowing truth comes from abiding (making our home) in the word of God. If we take up residence in the written word, we will come to understand the truth, and the truth we know will set and keep us free. This is the reason Satan tries so hard to keep us from the written word of God. He knows the written word will bring us face-to-face with the Living Word. This will make it so much harder for him to confront and conceal truth from us. Far too many people are being destroyed today because they have believed the devil's lie about the trustworthiness of the holy scriptures. It is shocking to hear what is being taught in many pulpits today from people who claim to be Christians. If what you are hearing taught goes against the written word of God—run! This is why bending and twisting the word of God is the most dangerous of all the warning signs.

If Satan is successful in confronting and concealing truth, he knows the ground is fertile to sow seeds of contradiction. "*You won't die!*' the serpent replied to the woman" (Genesis 3:4 NLT; emphasis added). The devil comes right out and contradicts what God said. What did God tell Adam would happen if he chose to eat from the forbidden tree? Here is the answer. "The Lord God placed the man in the Garden of Eden to tend and watch over it. But *the Lord God warned him*, 'You may freely eat the fruit of every tree in the garden—except the tree of the knowledge of good and evil. *If you eat its fruit, you are sure to die*'" (Genesis 2:15–17 NLT; emphasis added). The devil audaciously contradicts what God said—"You won't die."

This is where a large percentage of people who claim to be new creations in Christ have gotten to. They are openly proclaiming they are preaching the will of God even though it clearly goes against the word of God. This is deception in its fullest form. The reason deception is so dangerous is because it is so deceiving. You might want to give that sentence another read.

The next sound heard in the Garden of Eden was not the voice of the serpent. It was a loud "crunch." "So when the woman saw that the tree was good for food, that it was pleasant to the eyes, and a tree desirable to make one wise, *she took of its fruit and ate. She also gave to her husband with her, and he ate*" (Genesis 3:6 NKJV; emphasis added). It was the crunch that was heard around the world, and throughout eternity. The enemy's work was done.

The serpent could not force Adam and Eve to eat the fruit from the forbidden tree. All he can do is confront truth, conceal truth, and contradict truth. Eating the fruit is an act of a person's free will.

This is the inception of spiritual COVID. It was deadly then, and it can be life ending today.

THE WORD OF GOD GETS VERY LITTLE SCREEN TIME

How much time are you spending on Facebook compared to the time you're spending in the Faith Book (holy scriptures)? What if you received from the Holy Spirit, an alert about how much screen time you spend in God's word like you get on your electronic devices. What do you think you would discover? I am guessing it would be a shocking, sobering revelation. Just saying—

Have you noticed that we are not easily distracted when we are googling, texting, channel surfing, taking selfies, or casually flipping through our Facebook accounts. We can go for hours dawdling with our iPhones and never get distracted. But when it comes to spending quality time in the word of God, we are easily drawn away. Why is that? I'm glad you asked.

The enemy of our souls knows that the word of God is truth, and the more time we spend in the word—become intimate with the word— the better equipped we are to detect his attempts to confront, conceal, and contradict what God says. The more we know what God says about anything makes it so much easier for us to detect a lie that is being propagated as truth.

THE WORD OF GOD WILL READ YOUR MAIL

"For *the word of God is alive and powerful.* It is sharper than the sharpest two-edged sword, cutting between soul and spirit, between joint and marrow. *It exposes our innermost thoughts and desires.* Nothing in all creation is hidden from God. *Everything is naked and exposed before his eyes,* and he is the one to whom we are accountable" (Hebrews 4:12–13 NLT; emphasis added). We see from these two verses why so many people will not spend time in the written word of God. When you begin reading the word, it does not take long before you become aware that the word is reading you.

The writer begins with the written word of God, verse 12; then in verse 13, a shift is made to the Living Word (Jesus). Here, we are given the purpose of the holy scriptures: To bring us face-to-face with the Living Word to whom all of humanity is accountable. Many people (knowingly or unknowingly) will not spend much personal time in the written word of God on their own because the word has the tendency to make them uncomfortable knowing God sees and knows everything about them. A secret sin on earth is an open scandal in heaven.

If we do not get our information from the scriptures, the only alternative we have is to get our spiritual insight from other sources. If these sources are not grounded in the written word of God, if truth is based on their opinions or experiences, we have opened ourselves up to be deceived in believing a lie is the truth. If you ever hear these words spoken by the person you have given permission to speak into your life, "I know what the Bible says, but," remove yourself as quickly as possible, and do it in the spirit of grace. You are being set up by the enemy so he can infect you with spiritual COVID.

THE WORD OF GOD HAS NEVER CHANGED AND WILL NEVER CHANGE

The written word will never change because the one who spoke it never changes—the Living Word (John 1:1). Because God has no beginning, nor does he have an ending, his word will always remain the same—unaltered. "A voice said, 'Shout!' I asked, 'What should I shout?' Shout that people are like grass. Their beauty fades as quickly as the flowers in a field. The grass withers and the flowers fade beneath the breath of the Lord. And so it is with people. The grass withers and the flowers fade, *but the word of our God stands forever*" (Isaiah 40:6–8 NLT; emphasis added). The word of the Lord is the only vaccine against spiritual COVID that has proven to be efficacious and safe.

When we choose to take our stand on the word of God, we will forever be standing on a solid foundation. In this earthly realm storms will still come, the winds will continue to blow, hard days are going to challenge us, but we will not be moved, because we are standing on the unmovable Rock. This is the only way we can remain spiritually healthy in a sin-sick world.

GOD'S WAY OR THE HIGHWAY; WE HAVE A CHOICE; CHOOSE WISELY

A progressive movement today promotes the proposition that the church must be willing to accept the lifestyles of those who are clearly violating the word of God. Our world is changing, and we must be willing to change with it, they say. The word of God must make the same adjustment. We must be tolerant. After all, God is love. Those who refuse to compromise the word of God for the sake of societal transitions will be convicted of not loving people—without a trial.

The opposite is true. Loving people is the reason we warn them about the fate that awaits those who have chosen to go man's way and not God's. What if I heard you tell your child not to play in the street, and I said to you, "You don't love your child. If you did you would allow them the freedom to play wherever they want." I'm sure you would look at me, and say with emphasis, "I'm warning them about playing in the street because it is dangerous: It could cost them their lives." This is a great answer because it is true. You warn your children about playing in the street because you do love them. I would be totally out of order to say you don't love your kids because of the restrictions you place on them. There can be grave consequences for disobedience.

Because Jesus has all authority, he is the only one who can change the word of God. And this will never happen. "And Jesus came and spoke to them, saying, '*All authority has been given to Me in heaven and on earth*'" (Matthew 28:18 NKJV; emphasis added). Jesus will never use the authority that has been given him to bend and twist the word to accept what God condemns. "I don't speak on my own authority. *The Father who sent me has commanded me what to say and how to say it.* And I know his commands lead to eternal life; so *I say whatever the Father tells me to say*" (John 12:49–50 NLT; emphasis added). The individual who chooses to change or alter the word of God to mesh with society's progressive ideologies is usurping authority that does not belong to them. They are playing in the street, and there will be a huge price to pay.

What God said yesterday is still true today, and here is something you can rely on: it will be true tomorrow. His word never changes because he never changes. The written word is his breath. "*Every part of Scripture is God–breathed* and useful one way or another— showing us truth, exposing our rebellion, correcting our mistakes, training us to live God's way. Through the Word we are put together and shaped up for the tasks God has for us" (2 Timothy 3:16 TPT; emphasis added). God transmitted his very essence into his word. This verse clearly reveals why there is such a push to conform the word of God to today's ungodly lifestyles. The written word is God-breathed. It shows us truth. It exposes our rebellion, and it corrects our mistakes. That puts a damper on living the way we want to. Bending and twisting the scriptures to fit our opinions is demonic to the core. Just because we have laws and pass legislation to accept certain forbidden behaviors that are clearly condemned in the word of God does not mean it is the will of God. This would be a good place to say what I have already said several times. It is never the *will* of God if it goes against the *word* of God.

"*I am God—yes, I AM. I haven't changed.* And because I haven't changed, you, the descendants of Jacob, haven't been destroyed. You have a long history of ignoring my commands. You haven't done a thing I've told you. Return to me so I can return to you, says God-of-the-Angel-Armies" (Malachi 3:6–7 PTP; emphasis added). Since God transmitted his very essence into his word, and he never changes, neither does his word. If God says something is wrong, it will never be right no matter who says it is. To ignore this truth is very dangerous because it is a sure warning sign that spiritual COVID is present.

GOD'S WORD IS THE ONLY PLUMB LINE FOR A HAPPY AND HEALTHY LIFE

What is a plumb line? Merriam-Webster defines a plumb line this way: "A line (as of cord) that has at one end a weight (such as a plumb bob) and is used especially to determine verticality." Let me add to Merriam-Webster's definition of a plumb line: It can also be used to measure depth.

God gave the prophet Amos a picture of what a plumb line is and what it is used for. Amos may be referred to as one of the twelve minor prophets, but he gives us some major insights into what a plumb line is and why it is needed. Here is the vision God gave Amos. "Then he showed me another vision. I saw the *Lord standing beside a wall that had been built using a plumb line. He was using a plumb line to see if it was still straight.* And the Lord said to me, 'Amos, what do you see?' I answered, 'A plumb line' And the Lord replied '*I will test my people with this plumb line.* I will no longer ignore all their sins. The pagan shrines of your ancestors will be ruined, and the temples of Israel will be destroyed; I will bring the dynasty of King Jeroboam to a sudden end'" (Amos 7:7–9 NLT; emphasis added). In this vision, Amos sees God using a plumb line to judge the verticality of a wall that had been built by using a plumb line to establish its integrity. The plumb line doesn't move or change positions. It determines if everything else is in its proper place.

Since this is a vision, we know that the wall is not actually a wall, and the plumb line is not a literal one. The wall represents the standard God established in the very beginning of time for people to live by. His standard has never changed, and it never will. The plumb line in this vision is a symbol of truth and rectitude of conduct. In other words, it is the quality or state of being morally straight. Moral uprightness, inculcates that integrity of life and undeviating course of moral uprightness, which alone can distinguish a good and just person. Our lives remain straight and true when we are in agreement and harmony with the word of God.

Remember the sign over the blacksmith's shop we began this chapter with: "Bending and Twisting Done Here." Full-blown spiritual COVID has weakened the church because we have ignored this dangerous warning sign. We have gotten away from the plumb line—the word of God. The results are very noticeable. The church has gotten a mile wide and an inch deep. Don't forget that a plumb line measures depth as well as verticality.

Instead of demanding that our experiences come into line with God's word (the plumb line), we are guilty of dumbing down the truth to support our experiences. Instead of demanding that our lives (the wall) get back in line with God's word, we are bending and twisting (God's word), the plumb line, so it will fit our theological positions. To do this is telling God that he is a liar, and his word cannot be trusted. Since he won't allow his word to be changed to accommodate what we believe, we change his word to fit our narrative.

This would be a good time for us to sit quietly and listen attentively to what God told Amos in the vision he was given: "I will no longer ignore their sins." When God says something, he doesn't stutter like Moses did. He speaks clearly and succinctly. We never have to wonder what he says. To ignore this warning can be very costly—just ask Amos and the people he shared his vision with. It is the same warning we had better pay attention to. God is not practicing medicine without a license. He is the Great Physician.

"When Jesus heard this, he told them, 'Healthy people don't need a doctor—sick people do. I have come to not call those who think they are righteous, but those who know they are sinners'" (Mark 2:17 NLT). The Great Physician knows everything about everything; therefore, he knows his word is the only thing that will keep our lives straight (plumb) in a crooked world.

Anyone who chooses to measure moral straightness with anything other than the word of God is using the wrong standard. Never forget what God told Amos in his vision. He will use the plumb line (his word) to determine their spiritual verticality. He will no longer ignore their sins. The more we drift away from God's word, the more morally compromised we become. Unless we come back to the word of God as our guiding compass, it is only a matter of time before we are lost in a sea of immorality.

THERE IS ONLY ONE SURE FOUNDATION TO BUILD ON

In Paul's first letter to the Corinthian church, he too talks about the importance of building our lives on a sure foundation. A building's integrity is dependent on the foundation on which it sits. A construction contractor must never skimp on the materials used to build a solid foundation because it is the load-bearing part of a building. The life of a structure will be determined by what it sits upon.

Once again, Paul, like Amos, is not talking about a literal building. He is talking about our personal lives as children of God. The only lives that will survive time and eternity are the ones built on Jesus Christ, who is our sure foundation. This is why drifting away from the word of God as the standard for living, no matter how slightly, is setting us up to be overtaken by spiritual COVID.

The immaturity of the church in Corinth was exposed when they started arguing among themselves about who they thought was the best Bible teacher. One group was saying their man was Apollos; others were saying their number one pick was Paul. They had gotten away from the main thing. This is what Paul is addressing in the third chapter of his first letter to the Corinthians. Their attention had shifted. No longer was the foundation (Christ) in the crosshairs of their focus: personalities had become more important to them than anything.

Paul redirects their attention back to where it needs to be—on the foundation. "Or, to put it another way, *you are God's house*. Using the gift God gave me as a good architect, I designed blueprints; Apollos is putting up the walls. Let each carpenter [Christian] who comes on the job take care to build on the foundation! *Remember, there is only one foundation, the one already laid: Jesus Christ*. Take particular care in picking out your building materials. Eventually there is going to be an inspection. If you use cheap or inferior materials, you'll be found out. The inspection will be thorough and rigorous. You won't get by with a thing. If your work passes inspection, fine; if it doesn't, your part of the building will be torn out and started over. But you won't be torn out; you'll survive—but just barely" (1 Corinthians 3:9:15 TPT; emphasis added).

The devil is extremely skillful in using distractions to get us to go off the rails. If he can get us to shift our focus off Jesus Christ (our foundation) and the authority of his word (plumb line), we become easy prey. Once again, this is why doubting the word of God (which is the only thing that can keep our lives upright and stable), is the most dangerous warning sign that spiritual COVID is present, along with all its variants.

The inspection Paul mentions in this passage is underway right now. The Inspector is on the scene. "You do realize, don't you, that *you are the temple of God*, and *God himself is present in you*? No one will get by with vandalizing God's temple, you can be sure of that. God's temple is sacred—and you, remember, are the temple. Don't fool yourself. *Don't think that you can be wise merely by being up-to-date* [woke] *with the times*. Be God's fool—that's the path to true wisdom. *What the world calls smart, God calls unwise.* It's written in Scripture, He exposes the chicanery of the chic. The Master sees through the smoke screens of the know-it-alls" (1 Corinthians 3:16–20 TPT; emphasis added).

I have said this three or four times already, but it needs to be screamed from the highest rooftops as loudly and as long as it takes for the body of Christ to wake up: If what you are hearing taught goes against the *word* of God, it is not the *will* of God. It never has been, nor will it ever be. "Depend on it: God keeps his word even when the whole world is lying through its teeth. Scripture says the same: Your words stand fast and true; Rejection doesn't faze you" (Romans 3:4 TPT).

Demonic forces have increased their efforts to deceive the nations in this last season, even the elect if possible. I have been defining deception this way for many years: deception is dangerous because it is so deceiving. Those who are deceived are not even aware of it, or they believe that it is impossible for them to be deceived. In this last season it is imperative that believers stay alert, be aware of the enemy's tactics, and stay in the word. Truth can be found only in the word of God. "Jesus said to the people who believed in him, '*You are truly my disciples if you remain faithful to my teachings. And you will know the truth, and the truth will set you free*'" (John 8:31–32 NLT; emphasis added). When we make our home in God's word, we will be able to recognize counterfeit teaching in a nanosecond. Whatever you do, don't forget, deception is dangerous because it is so deceiving.

Excavation and foundation contractors, painters and carpenters rely on the plumb line to make sure everything is square and straight, giving a structure more stability, and increasing its life span. The foundation that we build our personal lives on is Jesus and Jesus alone. His word is the plumb line that keeps us aligned with truth and makes us impervious to spiritual COVID.

CONCLUSION

Christians who are *normal* in this last season will appear as being *abnormal* to those who are *subnormal*. How do other believers see you? How do you see believers who appear to be different than you? Do you see them as subnormal, normal, or abnormal? Do you think they are so heavenly minded they are of no earthly good? An honest answer to these questions may give you some insight into how you view this last season we have entered—if we have entered the last season. I am convinced we have.

We know that Christ is going to return because he promised he would. One thing is for certain, we are closer to his return today than we were yesterday. There are days when I think I hear Gabriel warming up the Lord's trumpet (1 Thessalonians 4:13–18 NKJV).

If what you have read in this book seems to be in another orbit, maybe this would be a good time to pause and give some thought to the challenge or threat it has made to your spiritual comfort zone. If it does present a threat, then it is perfectly legitimate to ask why? I will confess, there was a time in my ministry (early on) I would have had a hard time wrapping my mind around what I experienced in Uganda. But what we saw and experienced in Uganda is not unique to Africa; it is true in America. Everything I saw there I have seen here. What God did there he does here. He is God, and he does not change (Malachi 3:6 NKJV).

NEW NORMAL FOR THE LAST-SEASON CHURCH

The institutional church will carry on as it always has in this last season. Meetings will continue to follow prescribed schedules. Routine rituals and traditions will be guarded with ferocious vigor. Cold formality will continue unabated because procedure is more important than reason. If this is your spiritual restaurant of choice—bon appétit.

But God, a fresh wildness for the things of the Spirit of God is breaking out all over the world. This is so exciting to see and to be a part of. Once a child of God tastes the fresh fire of the Spirit, it does not take long for him or her to lose a taste for cold formality. Religious ritual cannot compete with or quench spiritual fire. God still fills the hearts of the hungry with good things (Luke 1:53 NKJV).

In this last season, a hungry heart will not be satisfied with religious crumbs. The diet for a child of God is milk, meat, manna. We will never outgrow our need for milk. The milk of the word is necessary for our spiritual health. We also need the meat of the word to mature and develop in our faith. But we are now in a season where hungry children of God will be feasting on manna. "Then Jesus said to them, 'Most assuredly, I say to you, Moses did not give you the bread *(manna)* from heaven, but My Father gives you the true bread *(manna)* from heaven. For the bread of God is He *(Jesus)* who comes down from heaven and gives life to the world'" (John 6:32–33 NKJV; emphasis added). "And Jesus said to them, 'I am the bread *(manna)* of life. He who comes to Me shall never hunger, and he who believes in Me shall never thirst'" (John 6:35, NKJV; emphasis added). We have entered a season where Jesus will be the main course on a hungry heart's menu. He is still filling hungry hearts with good things (Luke 1:53).

What we experienced in Uganda can happen in our services each week here in America. The reason we don't is not because we do not believe it can happen. We just don't expect it to happen. Can you imagine the experiences the church would have today, if the atmosphere where we assemble was bathed in belief and expectation? We would have to begin a new group on a weekly basis. The church of the Lord Jesus Christ is filled with hungry people who have become disgruntled with formality without faith, structure without substance, information without intimacy, rules without relationship, and performance without power.

This last season will be filled with opportunities for believers to step out of their comfort zones just like Peter stepped out of the boat onto the raging sea. The fear that had been in his face was now under his feet. Peter walked on the very thing others sink in. The rest of the disciples had the same opportunity Peter had but chose to stay inside the boat. This is a picture of the church in this last season. Some will be willing to risk it all and step out of their comfort zones into areas where they have no experience. They will encounter the miraculous when they do. Others will make the choice to stay in the boat of familiarity. Will you be a water walker or stay in the boat with your floaties on? You have free will, so it will be your choice. The Spirit of the Lord will give us many opportunities in this last season to *step out* of our comfort zones.

The church today can rise and be everything God intended for it to be. A controlled burn is going on within the church. The purpose for this controlled burn is not to destroy the church because the church cannot be destroyed. It is to release the church to be what the Lord had in mind since the beginning. It has taken the fire to get our attention. The true church is rising in power and with purpose. The church may be in its final season here on the earth, but more can be accomplished in these last days than we can imagine. We just need to be aware of what is going on and redeem the time.

This is not a time to be a spectator. Those days are over. It is time to rise, roll up your sleeves, and jump in with both feet. God wants to use you in ways you never dreamed possible. Age and gender are not limitations either. You may have to experience a controlled burn so the things that you have found security in are no longer available to you. I assure you, it will not be comfortable, but it will be liberating. If you are a child of God, you are living in the most exciting of times. If you are not a child of God, this would be a good time to get that settled by accepting and receiving Jesus as your personal Lord and Savior.

We have entered the season where God is revealing that every church is not the Lord's church, but he has his church in every church. The church is waking up. Miracles, signs, and wonders will be following those who believe (Mark 16:17 NKJV). God is going to take those of us who want to participate out of our comfort zones into zones where the Holy Spirit is our only comfort (2 Corinthians 1:3–4 NKJV). The supernatural is going to become natural to those who have the audacity to believe and to those who expect it.

Amid hostility and unbelief Paul and Barnabas stayed in Iconium for a long time preaching boldly about the grace of God. The Lord proved their message was true by giving them power to do miraculous signs and wonders (Acts 14:3 NLT). "Jesus Christ is the same yesterday, today, and forever" (Hebrews 13:8 NKJV).

The church is waking up! God has extubated his legitimate body (the true church) in this last season. It is time to stretch, yawn, and step out in faith—believing and expecting God to do the inexplicable. I am looking forward to seeing you on the wild side.

ABOUT THE AUTHOR

Wayne is married to his best friend, Betty Ann Kniffen. He has been a senior pastor for fifty years. For the last twenty-three years, Wayne and his wife, B. A., have lived in the Panhandle of Texas where he serves as a senior pastor, writes, and mentors pastors and church leadership teams. He serves as a geographical elder for several ministries, providing spiritual covering, vision oversight, and prayer support.

Wayne is known for his insight into new creation identity and has become an avid writer. His book *The Scam* deals with a believer's true identity in Christ. This book is a crucial read for Christians because most people are victims of identity theft. and they are not even aware of it.

In his book *The Exchange: God's Quid Pro Quo*, Kniffen talks about how we got our new creation identities. He explains it this way: *The Scam* teaches us about our true identities in Christ; *The Exchange: God's Quid Pro Quo* reveals to us how we got our new creation identities in Christ. Many churches, Bible study groups, life cells, are using these two books for their curriculum to teach on new creation identity.

If We Only Knew: Ignorance May Not Be Bliss is a must read for every believer. Kniffen contends that if we say that we believe right, but we are behaving wrong, we are living in deception. When we start believing right, especially when it comes to who we are in Christ, we will start behaving right.

The Prodigal Seen Through the Eyes of the Father deals with how God sees you, feels about you, and thinks about you. No matter how badly you may have blown it by making foolish choices, God is not mad at you. Your heavenly Father is madly in love with you.

New Creation Thinking—Living Life from the Inside Out provides great insight into how a successful Christian life is to be lived: it is to live life from the inside out not from the outside in. It is a thought-provoking explanation of ways born-again Christians should strive to live up to their full potential as new creations in Christ. It warns against becoming complacent and falling back into old habits that do not serve God's purpose.

All Kniffen's books have been published by WestBow Press.

Kniffen is gifted with the ability to take something that is simply profound and make it profoundly simple. He is known for his humor and quick wit. One of his best-known quotes is: "People will swallow more truth if they can laugh it down."

"A merry heart does good, like medicine" (Proverbs17:22 NKJV).

Personal contact:
<u>waynekniffen@outlook.com</u>

Website for Kniffen's books:
wkniffen.com

Printed in the United States
by Baker & Taylor Publisher Services